Psychology
of
Champions

Psychology
of
Champions

How to Win at Sports and Life
with the Focus Edge of
Super-Athletes

JAMES J. BARRELL, PH.D. AND
DAVID RYBACK, PH.D.

Foreword by Gordie Howe

Westport, Connecticut
London

Library of Congress Cataloging-in-Publication Data

Barrell, James J.
   Psychology of champions : how to win at sports and life with the focus edge of super-athletes / James J. Barrell and David Ryback ; foreword by Gordie Howe.
      p. cm.
   Includes bibliographical references and index.
   ISBN-13: 978-0-313-35436-6 (alk. paper)
   1. Sports—Psychological aspects. 2. Success—Psychological aspects. 3. Achievement motivation. 4. Athletics. I. Ryback, David. II. Title.
   GV706.4.B36 2008
   796.01—dc22   2008008015

British Library Cataloguing in Publication Data is available.

Library of Congress Catalog Card Number: 2008008015
ISBN-13: 978-0-313-35436-6

First published in 2008

Praeger Publishers, 88 Post Road West, Westport, CT 06881
An imprint of Greenwood Publishing Group, Inc.
www.praeger.com

Printed in the United States of America

⊚™

The paper used in this book complies with the
Permanent Paper Standard issued by the National
Information Standards Organization (Z39.48–1984).

10 9 8 7 6 5 4 3 2 1

Every reasonable effort has been made to trace the owners of copyright materials in this book, but in some instances this has proven impossible. The authors and publisher will be glad to receive information leading to more complete acknowledgments in subsequent printings of the book and in the meantime extend their apologies for any omissions.

Dedicated to all those who wish to optimize their performance in sports and life.

CONTENTS

Contents

FOREWORD

Life comes at you fast. It seems like a short time ago, I was on the ice, playing hockey among the greats—"Rocket" Richard, Bobby Hull, and many others. I loved playing the game. There was nothing like it. Now I'm known as Mr. Hockey.

When I played in the National Hockey League, every game was more exciting than the last. I played with a new perspective—from the eyes of the puck. That was one of my secrets, seeing the play from a more central viewpoint than my own. I got out of my own skin and into the center of the game that way. It worked great for me.

According to this book, many champions have some secrets that help get them to the top. The authors of this book, Jim Barrell and David Ryback, have searched out these secrets by talking with the champions in many sports—not only hockey but also baseball, basketball, football, golf, track, and others.

Never before has there been a book that got to the secrets or special "techniques" of champions by asking them directly, "What worked for you? How did you manage to get to—and stay!—at the top?" No other book has ever done this type of research and put it all together for the benefit of athletes, whether professional or amateur, for the benefit of coaches, whether at the high school, college, and even professional levels. I was impressed and amazed that so much valuable information on winning at sports could be put together in one book.

As I said, one of my secrets was to play by imagining I was seeing the rink from the eyes of the puck. For baseball great, Ted Williams, it was standing at the same place in the batter's box every time. For golf great,

Arnold Palmer, it was to attack the golf course rather than play it cautiously. For boxing champion, Joe Frazier, it was to fight like a warrior. For race car champ, Richard Petty, it was to be focused on the moment. For tennis great, Chris Evert, it was to never lose eye contact with the ball. You see, all of them had some secrets that helped them get to—and stay at—the top.

Jim Barrell and David Ryback refer to this as the Focus Edge—to put your focus where it counts, to get you to the edge of your performance. What a great concept! Somehow, the authors of this book were able to take all that information, based on their interviews with the champions over a number of years, and come up with the important points. I'm kind of glad they didn't come out with this book when I was still playing. It might have made the other hockey players a little too smart, if you know what I mean.

I loved the game of hockey so much, I couldn't imagine not playing. I wanted to play forever. Hockey was, and still is, in my soul. I was on four Stanley Cup-winning teams, and the only player to play over sixty years on the ice. I even played on the same team as my sons, Marty and Mark, for the Houston Aeros, New England Whalers, and Hartford Whalers from 1973 to 1980. Then, just to show them I was still around and kicking, I came back in 1997, to play with the Detroit Vipers. Now, in 2008, I can still feel the rush of adrenaline whenever I watch a game. Hockey is, and always will be, in my blood.

I want to finish by telling you that the important thing for winning at sports, and even in life, is to do the job and focus on the goal. As I once told my son, Marty, keeping two eyes open and your mouth shut is a great way to learn. As you read this book, learn all you can, take what works for you and, whatever your sport, practice, practice, practice. When I was a youngster, I watched the hockey greats and copied what they did and practiced those skills. That built my confidence. You can do the same but, instead of taking all the time to watch so many athletes, they're right here, in their own words, in this book, for you to learn from.

So go and be your best, as you learn from the champions.

Mr. Hockey®, Gordie Howe

PREFACE

1984—the sweltering Joe Louis Arena: At the fifth game of the first round of the NBA play-offs, the Detroit Pistons are being beaten by the New York Knicks. Suddenly, as the last quarter begins to fade into history, Isiah Thomas flashes into action, his moves flowing smoothly and electrically into flying perfection. Within a magical 94 seconds, he scores an incredible 16 points, forcing the game into overtime. "I remember coming back into the huddle at one time," he recalls, "and practically crying because everything was flowing so right."

What a moment—wanting the win so bad, you give everything you have! Everybody wants to win. Not only players and coaches—also the fans, management, owners, the media. Winning drives attendance, salaries, eventually … fame.

So what is the essential difference between a first place championship and finishing second? In many cases, a fraction of a second when speed determines, a point or two in events when skill determines. That small difference typically has less to do with physical stamina or skill than it does with mind or attitude. The mindset that puts the athlete into the winning zone, as we discovered after interviewing many successful super-athletes and sports legends, and recently using it to help the coaching staff that put the Florida Gators at the top of NCAA basketball for both '06 and '07, has certain characteristics across the board. We call it the Focus Edge.

Sports permeate our culture. In particular, we want to know who won and who lost. Those of us who are particularly interested in the art of winning want to know the secrets to success. This book deals with exactly that.

The "secrets" are revealed by the sports legends and super legends themselves from their own point of view. From the legendary Ted Williams to more contemporary athletes such as Michael Jordan and Wayne Gretzky, we discover that it's not necessarily physical superiority but rather a particular set of psychological factors that go into winning. Motivation, confidence, and concentration are all part of it, but only by hearing the athletes speak in their own words do we get the full sense of what the Focus Edge is all about.

Let's hear what Muhammad Ali had to say about his championship bout with George Foreman:

> Only a man who knows what it is to be defeated can reach down to the bottom of his soul and come up with the extra ounce of power it takes to win when the match is even. I know George wants to keep the champion's crown. He wants the crown, but is he willing to pay the price? Would he lay out his life?
>
> It's time to go all out. Toe to toe. George pours out a long left, and I cross my right over it. Now I've got to lay it all down on the line. If the price of winning is to be a broken jaw, a smashed nose, a cracked skull, a disfigured face, you pay it if you want to be King of the Heavyweights. If you want to wear the crown, you can play it careful only until you meet a man who will die before he lets you win. Then you have to lay it all on the line or back down and be damned forever."[1]

What about motivation? Both Ali and Foreman had it. Confidence? Both had to have it. Concentration? One had just a bit more—and that's all it took.

How was Jim Ryun able to beat the 4-minute-mile barrier when all about him were failing to do so? How did Wayne Gretzky rewrite hockey history by winning so many awards? What made Jack Nicklaus so persistently successful over the years?

What they all had in common was the Focus Edge, giving them the winning advantage. "Confidence is believing in my ability, knowing that I can do what I have to do to win," according to Jack. "Preparation is the key.... I might play for ten days prior to a major championship so I would know the golf course. I didn't leave anything to chance.... When I knew I was prepared, then I felt that I had an edge up on everyone else." He continued:

> The bottom-line reason why I played golf, I wanted to be the best at what I could do ... a game that I felt was the toughest game I'd ever played.... I felt that nobody could master it. There is no way that anybody is ever going to be 100% at it. Nobody ever has and nobody ever will.... I am motivated to get as close as I can to perfection.

So how do you get your mindset to win over others, especially under the pressure of champion competition, we asked Jack. "If I'm not driving the ball very well for some time," he answered, "if my swing is not so good, then I've got to figure out how I'm going to play off the tee so I can let other parts of my game work. If I'm driving the ball well, then I've got to take advantage of that. I've got to figure out some way of taking advantage of whatever I can do that day."[2]

"To watch Nicklaus putt is to watch a diamond cutter at work," according to *Sports Illustrated* writer John Garrity, offering a perfect image of the Focus Edge—"three minutes of scrutiny and analysis followed by a single, sure stroke resulting in something sparkling."

This book is unique. It's the first book to take the actual, lived experiences of super-athletes and sports legends and, through systematic analysis, to arrive at a teachable Focus Edge mindset. This mindset covers the areas of motivation, confidence, concentration, and the ability to deal with pressure situations.

We interviewed super-athletes and sports legends from a wide variety of sports in addition to Jack Nicklaus: Ted Williams, Johnny Unitas, Mario Andretti, Barry Larkin, Jim Ryun, Gordie Howe, Julius Erving, Jerry West, Wade Boggs, Richard Petty, and many others. From these interviews we learned how the athletes mentally approached their sports—how they were motivated, where their confidence came from, how they concentrated, including the popular notion of the "zone," and their methods for dealing with pressure situations. Even though the super-athletes come from a wide variety of sports, they share a common approach to their elite performances—the Focus Edge mindset. Simple and easily taught, it is applicable to people from all walks of life as well as a broad range of performance situations.

Everyone wants to win, if not in sports, then in some other aspect of life. The Focus Edge mindset is the way to do it, not only according to the authors, but in the words of the sports legends and super-athletes who were able to win over the years in one sport or another, from childhood to maturity. If there are secrets to being in the zone, this is where to find them! Now the secrets are revealed, through the common themes arising in our interviews.

MOTIVATION

The strength of an athlete's willingness to put forth the effort to fulfill a goal is what makes up motivation. It involves inner discipline and a strong sense of commitment—over time. Expectations of success fuel this fierce drive toward pushing the outer edge of the envelope in terms of effort devoted to competing at one's highest level, especially when the going gets tough. Mickey Mantle was so focused on getting good hits that when he struck out, his frustration resulted in his almost always breaking a water cooler. "Go break a water cooler!" the fans would taunt whenever he struck out. Casey even fined him, as did the league eventually, but that never affected his Focus Edge motivation. A healthy combination of desire to succeed and fear of failure keeps the super-athlete at the cutting Focus Edge of winning. "Win the races," said Mario Andretti, "then win the battles, then the wars—always striving to the next level."

CONFIDENCE

This is a key ingredient, the essence of which is characterized by the words storming out of Muhammed Ali's mouth: "I am the greatest!" Confidence in one's ability and particular skills is what matters—the highest level of competition. Far beyond trying and hoping, Focus Edge confidence is sometimes aided by an athlete's spiritual beliefs. In any case, this faith in oneself is based on a consistent track record of successful performance history. As Michael Jordan once put it, "I know where it is and how to get there and what it feels like to go deep inside for that extra push or pull I might need."

CONCENTRATION

Focusing is what enables the super-athlete to transcend competing distractions and to hone in on the challenge of the immediate moment. The perceived world slows down, and the details of the process are sharpened into the clear focus of reality. This is what's commonly referred to as "being in the zone." Attention to the important details becomes effortless. In some sports, narrow focus plays its part, as when a batter focuses on the pitch and can see the seams of the ball as it rolls "slowly" toward him. In other sports, broad attention allows the player to be aware of the field of surround. This happens when a quarterback scans the field for the best receiver or when a Wayne Gretzky becomes keenly aware of his teammates around him as he looks to make one of his perfect passes. "I had good peripheral vision," Gordie Howe, another hockey great, told us, "but I also used different perspectives. I imagined seeing the goal from the 'eyes' of the puck."

This winning combination proves successful in team sports such as football, basketball, baseball, and hockey; in individual sports such as running and car racing; and in one-on-one sports such as boxing and tennis.

According to the athletes interviewed, effective performance was facilitated by

- expectations of success
- separating Big Goals from Little Goals
- getting immersed in the challenge
- driving for perfection in process rather than results
- grooming skills at successive levels
- excelling within one's known limits
- enjoying the success of the moment

Here's how the athletes expressed it.

IN BASEBALL

"I was precise at the plate. Stand in the same place in the batter's box every time. Picture a good ball to hit. Learn from each pitch."

—Ted Williams (on concentration)

"I don't try to shut out the crowd. I simply focus on my target and the crowd disappears."

—Barry Larkin (on confidence)

"Be a predator—pounce on the prey [ball] and hit it hard."

—Matt Williams (on motivation)

IN FOOTBALL

"I played with reckless abandon, like there was no tomorrow."

—Ray Nitschke (on confidence)

"… when I am in the process and in the flow, I feel like I am a part of everything. It's like a dance."

—Steve Kiner (on concentration)

"I want to be the best and take things to a new level—to do the undone, to show the unseen, to be creative."

—Deion Sanders (on motivation)

"To play in the manner I demanded of myself, I needed to forget about stats and cosmetics and free my mind of clutter. I didn't give a damn about trophies and things like that."

—Jim Brown (on concentration)

IN BASKETBALL

"Go full tilt with an explosive and reckless disregard for whoever or whatever stands in my way."

—Charles Barkley (on confidence)

"Your focus is crystal clear. You are seeing and you are feeling things before they really happen. You just instinctively feel and know what's ready to happen."

—Isiah Thomas (on concentration)

"I can always go and talk to the game. It's a place of refuge."
—Michael Jordan (on motivation)

IN TENNIS

"Concentration is an ability to live only in each moment, not one second in the past, not one second in the future."

—Chris Evert (on concentration)

IN GOLF

"The pressure of competition against fine holes and fine players makes me feel very much alive. Life is intensified and the efforts you make under those circumstances come to have a significance of their own."

—Jack Nicklaus (on motivation)

Effective individuals use the same Focus Edge attitude to compete successfully, as do the sports legends who describe it in *Psychology of Champions*. From leadership challenges to reaching team goals in record time, using this achievable three-part attitude can make you a "super-athlete" in your own field of endeavor.

Motivation: Take some time out of your stressed-out world and meditate on what's important to you. Take a walk alone or an easy drive on a road with no traffic and think about what's really important to you. What will matter to you in the long run? What will make life worth living in terms of where you put most of your effort? What are you good at? How do you "follow your ecstasy"? Once you get clear about that, your motivation will climb to unfamiliar levels. Doing what you're good at and what makes you feel most fulfilled is how best to get motivated for the success of which you are capable. Read how Michael Jordan acquired his intensity for competition, how Wayne Gretzky proved his natural talents to his doubters, and how Arnold Palmer learned to attack the course rather than play it cautiously.

"Why do I play the game?" "Chipper" Jones of the Atlanta Braves reflected. "I think team. I am an extension of team. I live to 'carry' the team."

Another baseball star, Brad Wilkerson, said, "Baseball is a game that you have to prove yourself every day, every at-bat, every pitch."

"I always enjoyed sports," said 1996 Heisman Trophy winner Danny Wuerffel. "I am very competitive and I mentally and physically challenge myself—test myself. In football, I enjoy the camaraderie—to be able to celebrate a national championship together."

Another Heisman Trophy winner, and then coach of the national champion Gators, Steve Spurrier, said: "I like to make it fun and not have the players worried about not making mistakes. I want them to enjoy the competition." Motivation, for him, was characterized by the big picture, not the short term: "The key to success, I feel, is taking it year by year—one year at a time. Sometimes you can go forward, other times sideways."

Some sports legends are motivated by their own heroes. Before passing away on March 11, 2006, in Atlanta, hockey legend, Bernard "Boom Boom" Geoffrion, revealed,

> Rocket Richard motivated me. I said to myself, Why can't I do the same thing? I was never afraid to practice, work overtime—always trying to perfect my shot. Never thought about money. I was so happy to be playing for the Montreal Canadiens, I wanted to play the game to the best of my ability. I wanted to be the best—among the best. If a guy on my team scored two goals, I wanted to score three. I said to myself, This guy is no better than me. I loved the whole thing—the crowd, the electricity.... The goal is to find your purpose! That used to motivate me so much, I was not afraid of anything.

Geoffrion was not the only athlete motivated by the hockey great, Richard. NHL All-Star Ilya Kovalchuk of the Atlanta Thrashers won the Maurice "Rocket" Richard Trophy in the 2003–2004 season by heeding his father's advice, "If you are going to do anything, be the best." Kovalchuk is determined to be the best, but he's humble as well. "I have lots to learn," he says. "I want to be better. That's the reason why I'm here practicing, watching videotapes. When I finish my career, I can say I'm complete."

> Confidence: Continued improvement on what you decide to focus on builds on itself over time. Nothing succeeds like success and soon you'll feel more confident that you thought possible. Garner all your strengths and then be your authentic self—totally. What is it that you, in all your uniqueness, can do that no one else can do? Only you have that particular set of skills and abilities that make you unique. Know yourself and know the challenge set before you. As a leader, being honest and fair-minded will get you the support from above and below and add greatly to your sense of self-confidence. As a team member, knowing how to communicate to others what you're good at and what you want to do—to make the best contribution—will again add confidence. Read how Ted Williams built his confidence on the little things, how Jack Nicklaus developed his confidence through preparation, how Deion Sanders learned his limits and focused on what he *could* do.

"I used bits and pieces of past successes ever since I was a child," "Chipper" Jones told us. "I am already good when I take the field. I go out there and take the field *knowing* what I can do."

"Preparation is the key for me," said Danny Wuerffel. "I practiced so much through the years that I moved from 'I can do it' to simply 'Do it.' When you've done something over and over, it becomes a part of you. It becomes second nature."

"Confidence," agreed Coach Spurrier, "comes from preparation. Years of success form a background to draw from."

Persistence is what built confidence for "Boom Boom" Geoffrion. "I always felt if I put my mind to it, I could do anything. I needed to learn English, so I would pick up the English paper and I kept trying to read it. Hard work and discipline are everything … it's always a matter of *desire*!"

Focus Edge was Geoffrion's partner throughout his career. "I was only 14," he recalled, "and this man [an assistant coach] takes my equipment and throws it out of the dressing room. He says to me, 'You will never make the National Hockey League. Go home!' This makes me mad. Wow! I am only a kid.... I think maybe I show that man something." Geoffrion emerged as one of the all-time scoring greats with 393 career goals with his unrelenting focus, most of them with the Montreal Canadiens during their heyday of Stanley Cup championships. His booming confidence—his nickname came from his powerful shots on goal—put him in the zone whenever the tension in the rink called for his skills. In his final game, he scored the first goal, assisted on the second, and scored the winner as Montreal won its third straight Stanley Cup. He was then able, with quiet pride, "to show that man he was wrong."

Confidence in the zone comes as a result of preparation. "I just go up there and swing," Brad Wilkerson told us. "It just feels so good. I just feel confident in my hand speed and my bat speed.... I am not thinking about anything—just being in one moment after another, relaxed. Each moment is a challenge in itself."

> Concentration: Learn from the super-athletes how to be in the zone, how to focus on the moment at hand so that you're not distracted from achieving the success of which you're capable. Being in the moment with your associates, subordinates, or superiors makes you a force to be dealt with. Being your authentic self as you are in the moment makes you worthy of others' respect and loyalty. You come across as more trustworthy and dependable. Read how Mario Andretti set out to control his mind around a single objective, how Gordie Howe saw the goal from the eyes of the puck, and how Chris Evert gained "an ability to live only in each moment, not one second in the past, not one second in the future."

The secret to concentration is to focus on the process, not the outcome, and to come prepared to win. "Concentration comes from being prepared," Coach Spurrier told us. "When you feel prepared, then you are confident and can focus on the game."

"If something becomes too important," said Danny Wuerffel, "you could worry and lose concentration. If I throw a touchdown or an interception, it doesn't change who I am. I am not what I do. I do take pride in what I do, but it is pride in doing things with all my strength...."

"Chipper" Jones' teammate, Greg Maddux, was, according to his performance coach, Jack Llewelyn, "like a surgeon. Plays the game totally within himself—real private. He thinks like the hitters he will face. Very businesslike in relation to his game. Plays for pride, not compensation."

"Boom Boom" Geoffrion was highly intense about his hockey, so intense that he couldn't sleep the afternoon of the game. So he'd go for a walk instead. "When I used to go to New York," he told us, "I would go to the Metropolitan Opera in the afternoon. The music opened me up and showed me the bigger picture. I loved it. I had plenty of intensity; what I needed was more perspective and relaxation to focus." Geoffrion softened the intensity of his Focus Edge by seeing the bigger picture, in this case, by immersing himself in the drama of opera.[3]

Being in the zone means focusing on the present moment with all your being. It means not being aware of anything else but what's in front of you—you and the game. Recent research, described in the best-selling book, *Blink,* by Malcolm Gladwell,[4] reveals that, when clearly focused, the body can react to demanding stress with "extreme visual clarity, tunnel vision, diminished sound, and the sense that time is slowing down." Gladwell goes on to tell us that "basketball superstar Larry Bird used to say that at critical moments in the game, the court would go quiet and the players would seem to be moving in slow motion."

For Brad Wilkerson, being a winner meant total concentration:

> I don't feel anything. There is no pressure. I am so confident.... Everything seems to be going real smoothly. The ball appears real big as it comes up to the plate. I am nice and quiet inside, and my hands just take over—it feels so good. I don't hear much from the fans the whole game—I block everything out. I am completely focused on trying to beat my opponent—nothing else. I play the game within myself.... So my concern is my game and not others' expectations of me.[5]

We hear so much about being in the zone during those exceedingly personal moments of successful competition. Olympian Jennifer Heil, World Cup mogul skier in 2006, described it this way: "To feel the speed of my skis racing over the moguls is addictive. When I soar through the air during my jumps, it is magical. Feeling my heart thumping in my chest makes me feel so alive."

Winning like a champion with the Focus Edge involves all these aspects and then some. It means going all the way with all that you can bring to the game. Forty-two-year-old Dean Karnazes,[6] author of *Ultramarathon Man*, has been outrunning everyone else since his 30th birthday. "I never feel more alive than when I'm really challenged and really struggling to do something." In July of 2004, he won the Badwater Ultramarathon, a 135-mile race through California's Death Valley, where temperatures reach as high as 125 degrees. It took him 27 hours to do it, but it took all the other runners even longer. What does being in the zone mean to Karnazes? "I've just learned that if I'm not following my heart, it's not worth it."

Following his heart meant the focus of pounding the pavement more than his competitors. In the end, it's all about preparing for the Focus Edge with practice. Paul "Bear" Bryant, college football's most successful coach with six national championships and 13 Southeastern Conference titles, probably said it best: "It's not the will to win that matters—everyone has that. It's the will to prepare to win that matters."

Winning as a champion has a price and the price is preparation and focus. Steve Alford, Olympic gold medalist, who played with Michael

Jordan on the U.S. Olympic team, had this to say about him: "There was a huge gap between his ability and the ability of the other great players on that team. But what impressed me was that he was always the first one on the floor and the last one to leave."

When all is said and done, winning with Focus Edge means the motivation to work hard from the beginning, the confidence that comes with preparation, and the concentration to focus all that hard-earned talent on each moment of competition. The sum total, when it culminates in what we call the Focus Edge, manifests in an unbeatable self-confidence that takes a champion all the way. It's the swagger in a Heisman Trophy winner; the quiet, flowing grace on ice of a Wayne Gretzky; the cool readiness of a slugger at bat. It's what Muhammad Ali meant when he proclaimed, "I'm the greatest!"

As Olympic gold medalist and professional tennis champion Venus Williams put it, "You have to believe in yourself when no one else does. That's what makes you a winner."

Way after the lights first flick on, after the crowds roar their support for their favorite athletes, when it's down to the dying minutes of a brutally fought tie game, the Focus Edge is what makes the difference. It may be a long set shot that bounces off the rim into the basket, a touchdown pass from the opposition's 40-yard line, or a single with the bases loaded. But that shot, pass, or hit makes all the difference in those last dire moments when the tension is as tight as it ever gets. The crowd erupts in an emotional outburst that creates lifetime memories for both athletes and fans alike—especially if it's a playoff or championship game. Being in the zone with the Focus Edge makes for the winning advantage. That's how the champions do it!

ACKNOWLEDGMENTS

No book is the product solely of its authors. There are many behind the scenes who, over the years of its development and writing, contribute to the final product. In our case, first and foremost, there are the athletes we interviewed who were generous with their time and sharing of their personal experience. What makes this book so unique is just that—the openness, both in heart and mind, of the sports legends and super-athletes who shared their philosophy of success, the "secrets" that helped them make their way to the top and stay there for a significant period of sports history. This sharing, hopefully, will pave the way for future generations of successful athletes, shaving years off their learning curve.

Beyond that are the individuals who supported us in their own unique ways. Nova Lanktree, an Executive Vice President at CSMG Sports, helped arrange most of the interviews. Don Medeiros, track coach at the University of Western Alabama, helped with the writing at one point in its development. James E. Barrell, son of the senior author, was part of the conceptualization of the book. Laura Sweeney helped track down the athletes, years after the interviews had been done, in order to get their releases. Suzanne Sindledecker helped with the editing. Carrie Sun provided invaluable computer, logistical, and other much needed support toward the end of the project, and when things got too serious or intense, Grace Ryback was always there to provide some much needed humor as relief.

When we met Debbie Carvalko, a senior acquisitions editor at Praeger, at a professional psychology conference, we knew we had met the right publisher after years of considering many. Debbie was positive about the project from the first moment of discussion about it, and she never stopped, being encouraging and supportive at every step. Her associate at Praeger, Brian Foster, was equally supportive whenever issues popped up.

INTRODUCTION

It's the sixth game of the NBA Championship Series and Michael Jordan is fatigued. He's been mercilessly hounded and punished by the Utah Jazz defense, in one of the most physical series in NBA history. Drenched with sweat, he pulls himself out onto the floor. The World Championship is riding on the next few seconds. Michael knows he will take the shot to win or lose the game. The Jazz knows he will take the final shot, and they will do anything to stop him. Thousands of fans are screaming their lungs out and millions across the globe are watching on television. Every major paper and magazine will cover this game. It's an historic moment. What is going through Michael Jordan's mind at this precise moment? What is he thinking that allows him to hit the game-winning shot, even in the face of a stifling defensive effort? How is he able to hit this NBA championship-winning shot, as he has hit so many game-winning shots before, in spite of the pressure and the fatigue?

Flash to another scene....

It's the 1988 Super Bowl and time is running out. The San Francisco 49ers are trailing the Cincinnati Bengals 16-13, and there's only 3:20 left in the game. Joe Montana calmly leads his team on a 92-yard drive to score the winning touchdown with only 39 seconds left. With a worldwide audience viewing perhaps the single most watched sporting event in the world, what is going through Joe Montana's mind as he attempts to lead his team to victory?

We have long been fascinated by the above questions. What is it about the super-athletes, the winners, that allows them to be so successful, especially under the most harrowing and difficult of situations? Finding answers to these questions is what we set out to do in this book, *Psychology of Champions*. For the first time ever, these answers have come from the world's greatest athletes themselves.

This book summarizes several years of research with some of the greatest athletes in the history of mankind. It was our intention to discover what it was about this very highly select group of athletes that separated them from their fellow competitors. Why were they able to experience such overwhelming success over a prolonged period of time? We knew, from the outset, that the explanation of their success and longevity could not be totally explained on the basis of physical talent alone. In fact, some of these athletes, clearly, did not have a corner on physical talent. Of course, they were physically gifted, when compared to most nonathletes. However, when compared to their fellow athletes, many were judged to be just average or a little above average. Some were even judged to be below average in raw physical ability. Yet, this group of athletes was able to consistently outperform most other players. They seemed impervious to pressure. In clutch situations, those win-or-lose, sudden-death-type situations, they were able to prevail more often than not. Why was this?

THE FOCUS EDGE MINDSET

Knowing that the explanation didn't lie so much in physical ability, we looked at what we called the "inside" game. We went directly to these sports legends and super-athletes—all sports legends were the super-athletes of their day—for their own descriptions and explanations of how they dominated their games. We looked for clues in the ways that they approached the mental side of their games. What did these players think about before a game, during a contest, or after competition was concluded? What did they believe about themselves and their opponents? What were their emotions like before, during, and after they competed? What was their concentration like? What types of goals did they set for themselves?

Take Jack Nicklaus, one of golf's superstars, for example:

> I wanted to be the best at whatever I was doing ... and still do. Realistically, I could never be the best at everything, but the key for me was that I strive for it. I loved all sports, and until I chose my career path in golf at age 19, I participated in all sports and wanted to be the best I possibly could in all of them. I made a pretty good basketball player, but I certainly didn't have the physical capabilities to be the best. At golf, I didn't need to be the biggest, strongest, or fastest. With golf, I enjoyed the fact that it was just me against

myself or me against the golf course. I didn't need someone to throw a ball to me or catch a ball or defend me to enjoy the game.

I love competition. I love preparing for competition.... I always felt like when I went to a major championship, I always went in feeling prepared. When asked over the years how I dealt with pressure, I responded that I dealt with pressure by being as prepared as possible for those situations.

Confidence comes from winning. I got beat when I was a youngster a few times but, as I kept playing, I found myself beating players older than me. As the competition became better, I played better. I always played better when I played someone better than myself.

I've never had a problem focusing. My wife has always kidded that I could be watching television and the house could burn down around me, without me knowing it. I've always been able to focus real hard on whatever I'm doing. I've always had to work on what I was doing and what I'm trying to accomplish. I never *let* things happen; I tried to *make* them happen.[1]

Focusing real hard seemed to be a key component of Nicklaus' game.

Interviews such as this one led us to understand that it was this "inside" game that would explain (at least in part) such dominance over golf, in this case. What we found was that this select group of super-athletes shared some very basic mental characteristics. They had a very definite way that they mentally approached their sports.

Here's how Ted Williams approached baseball:

I played the game for pride—to know I could do it as well as anybody. Money was important to me since I didn't have much as a child. Fear and motivation never went together for me. If I had fear, I would get mad. Fear was not part of my game.

When I was a youngster, I would be out late at night practicing my swing. During those early years, I didn't have confidence. I just *hoped* I could do it. I was ambitious and determined. I practiced and was thoughtful about what I was doing. Most importantly, is that I built on little things. Set small goals that I could do and accomplish.

In the early years, I was taught the inside-out swing. To be able to swing like that is darn important and gives you a big advantage. That was when I was hitting my very best. That swing—it's the wrists and the rest is follow-through. I hit very few ground balls and hit into very few double plays. I was very confident in my swing. I didn't think about being loose or swinging hard. I only thought about coming around quick. Mastering the swing is a key.

Who would have thought that the great Ted Williams lacked confidence as a youngster, and so practiced so much harder! He ended up focusing so sharply on what he calls the "inside-out swing." That single focus—as small a goal as it may have been—was key to his success as a hitter. He discovered the significance of conquering small goals, an important component of the Focus Edge mindset, as we'll find out.

Although super-athletes such as Ted Williams were not always successful, they did have an optimal mindset when they were. Their thoughts, beliefs, expectations, and emotions all seemed to converge into what we call the Focus Edge mindset. Here's how Ted manifested it:

> I had to be in the moment. Not only to be ready for a fastball but for self-preservation—to keep from getting hit. If you're not ready for a fastball, how in the heck are you going to get out of the way from it? The only pitch that you have to be ready for is a fastball. The quicker you are, the longer you can wait.
>
> If I could guess right on a pitch, I could hit it—I didn't give a darn who threw it or where it was. I would picture a good ball to hit. I would always look back and learn from the last pitch. I would say things like, "Geez, Ted, you weren't ready for that fastball." I was aware of short umpires calling low strikes and tall umpires calling high strikes.
>
> Be focused. Don't help the pitcher! Don't be distracted by how he looks. Like that Johnson. He was six-foot, nine—all arms and legs and threw like the devil. There was no one compared to him. I shudder when I think of him. However, he didn't have control. There was nobody who has ever played the game that had it all. I was aware of a pitcher's weaknesses. I was a student of the game.[2]

That's one champion's set of strategies—the Focus Edge mindset that put him in the top ranks of baseball heroes, keeping his focus on "a good ball to hit." For the first time, we are able to put it all together and see what super-athletes have in common when they are successful in their sport. This book is devoted to explaining and demonstrating this mental approach in athletic competition, which we call the Focus Edge mindset.

Along the way we also made another exciting discovery: The "inside" game of the world's best athletes was really something that anyone could do. The way these athletes thought about their sports (and their lives) was something that was surprisingly simple and, most important to us, *this Focus Edge mindset could be taught.*

Take, for example, Mario Andretti's Focus Edge on competition in racing cars:

> The event was very important to me, so it was easy to stay focused. Before a race, I needed my space to collect my thoughts, weed out distractions, control

the mind around a single objective. I became possessed about being excellent that day. When I was in "the zone," I was like in a trance. Time didn't exist. Things slowed down—only one objective—and all thoughts were on it.

When the pressure was on, I slowed down and reasoned things out. Indianapolis—two hundred fifty thousand people in the stands. My reasoning process went like this: "Car feels the same as it does when no one is there. This is my job. Just ignore everything else." I became arrogant to the situation. I wouldn't let the crowd or anyone interfere with me.... I loved the pressure. Without it, life was boring.[3]

Andretti's strategies work for winning on the race track. This approach of focusing on the ultimate goal can easily be taught, along with other aspects of the Focus Edge mindset.

We have directed this book at a general audience. Coaches, athletes, teachers, consultants, or anyone who loves sports and believes that there is value in athletic competition can find ideas of interest in these pages. For parents there are valuable ideas on how to look at their children's sports. If children can learn to use the Focus Edge mindset, they will most likely experience greater success in their athletic endeavors. More important, they also will become better equipped to deal with the challenges that life provides off the athletic field. The millions of amateur athletes in any sport will find help in the material we present. The weekend softball player, the X-treme games competitor, and the summer league bowler can all apply the discoveries we share in this book.

We also believe that the general reader, even if not a sports fan, will find value in these pages. Most of us will never play in a World Series and come to bat in the bottom of the ninth inning with a chance to make history. However, all of us face pressure situations in our day-to-day lives—financial worries, health concerns, relationship problems at home or work, or worries about where our lives are headed. We believe the Focus Edge mindset can help ordinary people deal effectively with ordinary, day-to-day problems. The principles of the Focus Edge mindset can be used in any setting, not just athletics. It offers sound principles for living.

EMOTIONAL INTELLIGENCE AND THE PSYCHOLOGY OF CHAMPIONS

As we interviewed with athletes and learned from other coaches and sports psychologists, we became aware of an important aspect of the psychology of champions. These have more to do with *emotional intelligence* rather than the performance perspective itself. Basically, emotional intelligence involves self awareness, self-discipline, awareness of others, and managing social situations. The learning we acquired can be consolidated along the following points:

1. Self-awareness through good and bad times: At some point in the athlete's life, there are bound to be self-doubts. The imposter syndrome takes over at times and creates feelings of guilt about accolades that may go far beyond one's actual abilities. The successful athlete must battle these negative emotions.

   RULE 1: As Popeye says: I yam what I yam. You're a successful athlete, even on bad days.

2. Emotional self-control: Along similar lines, the successful player needs to take athletic risks that may occasionally result in failure, often in public view. The Focus Edge must be stressed if continued success is sought. Such risk, with its inevitable occasional failings, is part of the price of playing at the top of one's game. Guilt and self-blame are often the result. Emotional self-control is the key and this is part of what supportive family and coaching can encourage.

   RULE 2: Occasional failure is part and parcel of being a top winner. At such times, remember who supports you—win or lose.

3. Social self-control: In the past couple years, there has been a growing awareness of the need for emotional self-control and presentation skills, under the title of "social intelligence." This is as true of the successful athlete as anyone else. These individuals need to learn to keep themselves on the right track—self-control: to present themselves to the public with a professional demeanor; to have some understanding of their role to the public, both in terms of their off-play behavior and of public appearances. Training in such topics as emotional and social intelligence is becoming more and more essential.

   RULE 3: You're a professional now, not a kid on the block. Act accordingly.

4. Personal self-control: The successful team athlete walks a thin line between being a super-athlete in his own right on the one hand, and being a team player on the other. Coaching style has a strong influence on this. There is no clear answer. A super-athlete stands out from the team, yet at the same time cannot succeed without the team. Where *personal identification* falls is an ongoing challenge, particularly for the top players. The best solutions seem to be a closer

identity with the team, allowing the media to create idol worship for their own commercial reasons.

RULE 4: Even when you feel like the greatest, you're nothing without your teammates.

5. Self-control under pressure: "Big events"—such as breaking ties in tight playoff games—can be life-altering experiences for the super-athlete, whether they end in failure or success. How often a career is marked by such critical moments, overshadowing a life-long career of forgotten details! The more successful athletes enter such dramatic moments relying on their past history of successful practices, rather than going over the edge to try something different. They appear to have that emotionally intelligent characteristic of self-management at such adrenaline-packed moments and, more than not, succeed because of that.

    RULE 5: At the moment of truth, do what you do best, and have done before. This is not a time for "stunts."

6. Self-discipline over the years: Success toward champion status requires more than practice. It involves living in a world that is often much less structured than that of the ordinary individual. Yes, practice is important, but typically over an extended period of time, often over a number of years. How does one manage one's life not only to get that practice in, but to keep persevering over the years? The successful athletes know the answer.

    RULE 6: Make your practice time a No. 1 priority.

7. Self-management: Universal for all super-athletes is the need for *constant feedback* in terms of Focus Edge performance. Standards of excellence are not easily available for top performers, as records continue to be broken over time. Best performance appears to come from a combination of good coaching feedback and a strong self-awareness of Focus Edge performance over the years. The best athletes know themselves well enough to push the envelope just so far.

    RULE 7: Stretch the envelope, but don't tear it to pieces. Learn your outer limits.

8. An awareness that coaches come in different forms: Good coaching is essential. Many successful athletes were lucky enough to have a parent as an excellent coach during the very formative years. Others received great coaching during high school. Some talented individuals didn't get the great coaching till college. But somewhere along

the line, a great coach has an important role to play on the road to success.

RULE 8: Coaches come and go—from childhood to high school and onward. Remember what your best coaches taught you, along with your present coach.

9. Awareness of the importance of support from home: The successful, young athlete plays for different teams as he changes schools, neighborhoods, etc. Later on, as the rookie becomes professional, there is constant travel and the inevitable transition from team to team. *Stability is essential*, and this is often in the form of supportive family and friends.

RULE 9: Remember where you're from. These folks don't change.

These findings are the result of discussions with other sports psychologists as well as observing super-athletes and their need for emotional intelligence. They are part of the psychology of champions from the perspective of the cutting edge of motivation, confidence, and concentration.

WHY WE'RE FASCINATED BY THE PSYCHOLOGY OF CHAMPIONS

We love sports. Some of our fondest childhood memories involve playing sports. It wasn't uncommon for us to be gone all day to a park or school ground, often playing several different sports in one day. During these easy, carefree days we often dreamed of playing professional sports. Baseball, football, basketball—it didn't matter. We imagined our exploits in the "pros." Like so many kids, we dreamed of hitting the game-winning shot as the clock wound down in the NBA finals or hitting a home run in the bottom of the ninth inning with the bases loaded to win the World Series.

We imagined ourselves to be our heroes—the super-stars of those days—whose statistics we memorized and whose every game we followed. We would argue over who got to be Hank Aaron or Willie Mays in our pick-up games. We would argue over who was the better player—Jerry West or Oscar Robertson, and we would sit spellbound as we watched them make plays that no one else could make. Even at that young age we had an awareness that there was something special, something different about our heroes that made them stand out, head and shoulders above the rest of the pack. We didn't know what it was that made them special and different, but they were.

To this day we still love sports. Although the games and the players have changed, we still have that same fascination with outstanding athletes. They still captivate us, perhaps even more so, now that we can appreciate the time and effort it takes to become a super-star. Now, however, instead of dreaming about "being a pro," our thoughts focus on that same childhood awareness of how "special" certain athletes are. We wonder why some athletes are "super" and others are not. Why is it that some athletes seem to be able to deliver in the clutch over and over again? Why is it that some athletes never seem to be able to deliver? Why were some of our heroes able to be so successful, time and time again? Are there any similarities between our heroes of yesterday and the super-stars of today that can account for so much success?

Do you enjoy sports? Do you enjoy playing or watching your favorite sport on weekends? Do you find yourself getting excited, nervous, frustrated, or angry when you play your favorite sport? Do you ever wonder why you feel this way? Perhaps you are among the millions who enjoy watching sports more than playing. Do you, like us, marvel at what great athletes are able to accomplish? Have you ever wondered why some athletes are consistently able to be so successful?

METHOD OF DISCOVERY

We believe it is important for you, the reader, to know how we discovered the Focus Edge mindset. First of all, there is the selection of the athletes. What is greatness in sports? Athletes can become legends. There are even special places like the Hall of Fame for baseball and football, where exceptional athletes can be remembered for their extraordinary performances. Superstars become household names. However, there are many super-athletes who do not enjoy this special attention and popularity, and this may have little to do with their performances and more to do with their circumstances and personalities. It was our task to place the emphasis on performance and pick and choose from this broad spectrum of elite athletes.

We have selected a sample of these super-athletes across different sports for this book. We had to decide what makes up a super-athlete. We settled on *dominance* and *consistency*. This does not mean that they need to completely dominate their game. What it does mean is that they are in control, in charge of their performance, and can be dominant at any time in a game situation. In basketball, it is "the go-to guy." In football, it is the guy you give the ball to as you approach the goal line. On some occasions, this super-athlete might even completely take over a game.

Because these athletes are not gods, they experience failures as well as successes. What really matters here, however, is the consistency of their successes over time. For example, for a hitter in baseball to hit .300 every year is exceptional. Here we are, talking about lasting over the long haul. Super-athletes put up superior numbers and performances year after year. This consistency is the true measure of their success. These are the kinds of athletes that we have chosen for this book.

We made an effort to find super-athletes in a wide variety of sports. We went beyond the "Big Three" (baseball, basketball, and football) and tried to learn from athletes in a wide variety of sports. It was our belief that only by including a wide variety of sports (and athletes) could we draw conclusions that we could then apply to a wide variety of situations. Over the period of several years, we conducted well over sixty interviews with super-athletes. Included were Ted Williams, Jack Nicklaus, Julius Erving, Johnny Unitas, Mario Andretti, Nancy Lopez, Gordie Howe, Joan Benoit, Jim Ryun, Wade Boggs, Deion Sanders, Richard Petty, Jerry West, and many others. Here, for example, is what we learned from hockey great, Gordie Howe, about his Focus Edge—on the future rather than the past—for motivation:

> My main goal was to play forever and break the record for longevity. I loved every aspect of the game. Challenge and competition were important. Always felt like the team was relying on me. I was focused on the future and not the past. I wouldn't worry about contracts and not care about past accomplishments, collecting awards, and things like that. I loved playing the game. I was very aggressive. Revenge was sometimes a factor. I would play hurt, like when I had a broken collarbone and kept it a secret. Somehow, when I didn't feel good physically, I played smarter.
>
> I never felt fear during a game. I would be very excited, not anxious, before a game, until the puck dropped. I couldn't wait to get started! I never even knew pressure was there until after the game was over.[4]

So what do we learn here that might contribute toward the Focus Edge mindset? Being motivated by the challenge of competition; the confidence to focus on team support rather than self concern, even to the point of physical pain; the desire to excel, to "play smarter" when slowed down by injury; and such concentration on the game that fear and anxiety were overshadowed by intense involvement. Despite the casual style of the words spoken, there is a depth of information here.

We also read hundreds of interviews with athletes from magazines and newspapers. Then we painstakingly pored over this wealth of material and looked for common elements that were shared by these elite athletes. We noticed that there were definite ways in which they differed from one another. But, in the end, we found that they did, indeed, share some very basic mental skills that were used to great advantage in their athletic careers. This became the Focus Edge.

Our definition of a super-athlete emerged as one who has demonstrated *consistent dominance* in his or her sport over a long period of time. There can, of course, always be arguments about who was really dominant or what constitutes a long period of time. However, we believe our list of super-athletes and sports legends is a fair and representative one. There are current athletes who might well, one day, be included in our sample. At the writing of this book, however, many had not yet dominated their sport for a sufficiently long period of time.

The biographical sketches of our chosen super-athletes and sports legends are organized according to sport at the back of the book.

ORGANIZATION

The book is organized in a simple and effective manner. This first chapter introduces the Focus Edge and the athletes who helped us discover it. Also discussed is the "inside-game," the game of the mind. You, the reader, will be able to look directly into the minds of numerous super-athletes and learn exactly what they were thinking and feeling while performing the amazing athletic feats that so often astounded us.

Sections I to III take a close look at the Focus Edge and its three stages. The super-athletes seemed to agree that *motivation, confidence,* and *concentration* were the most important ingredients in their success. Each of these three main components is discussed in detail. Numerous examples, taken directly from super-athletes, are given and then discussed. The fourth section discusses how the three main components are successfully used in *pressure situations*—one of the hallmarks of a super-athlete.

Each section ends with a short summary of what we discovered in the time we spent with the super-athletes. In the Summary we distill the Focus Edge that super-athletes use to achieve their success.

Overall, the book presents a unique methodology used to form conclusions for development of the Focus Edge. The information we obtained comes directly from the athletes themselves. Although most sport psychology books present material from experimental psychology, we have utilized a very different approach called experiential (*not* experimental) research.

This type of research focuses on the actual *experiences* of human beings as the source of its data and conclusions.

The information for this book was derived from the super-athletes and sports legends themselves—directly from how they experienced competition. Thus, the information is not from subjects who took part in an experiment in a laboratory far from a playing field. It is not from people who may have never swung a bat or thrown a pass. It is not from a theoretical statement about how people might behave some or most of the time. Rather, it is from the superstars themselves—as they lived their competitions. It shows how and what they thought—the mental approach they used to achieve dominant success over a prolonged period of time.

SECTION I: MOTIVATION

WHAT FUELS OUR FIRES

The year is 1958. The New York Giants are playing the Baltimore Colts for the World Championship. With 2 minutes remaining, the Colts are trailing 17-14 and have the ball on their own 14-yard line. With the crowd going wild, **Johnny Unitas** comes to the line of scrimmage and looks out at the best defense in the NFL. He barks out his signals. Few people in the screaming crowd know that he has three broken ribs and that he is wearing a corset made of steel and foam rubber. Despite these obstacles, he completes seven consecutive passes and drives the Colts to a game-tying field goal with 7 seconds remaining. In sudden-death overtime, battered, bruised, and exhausted, he leads the Colts on a 79-yard touchdown drive to win the World Championship, in what many consider the greatest pro football game ever played.

Johnny U. was not considered a top prospect when he came out of college. He was actually playing semi-pro football when he was offered the chance to compete in the NFL. Yet, he finished his career as one of the most celebrated quarterbacks ever to play the game. What motivated this athlete, judged to be of just average physical ability, and allowed him to become such a storied player and the hero of millions of fans? What is it that motivates super-athletes and allows them to rise above the level of their fellow players, many who are more physically talented?

To discover what motivates super-athletes, we asked them the following questions:

1. Why do you play the game? What is the essential reason?

2. What are your goals during competition?

Let's share what we learned from them. It is, first of all, important to know exactly what is meant by motivation. People use the term "motivation" in a wide variety of ways. It can mean many different things to many people. From our work with super-athletes as well as extensive research, we have defined motivation as the strength of the athlete's willingness to make the effort to fulfill a goal. There are three main parts of this definition: (1) the strength of an athlete's desire, (2) the effort needed to reach the goal, and (3) the goal to be fulfilled.

There are at least two sides to an athlete's *desire*. Notice, first of all, that this definition does not say the strength of the athlete's desire to fulfill a goal. Motivation is much more than that. Having a strong desire to reach a goal is certainly important, but it is not enough. This is where the second side of desire comes into play. An athlete can want something badly but still not be motivated to take the difficult steps necessary to achieve the goal. The road to athletic success can be long, tedious, and very difficult. There can be many ups and downs along the way. Super-athletes, as we will see, all have a strong desire to reach their goals. However, they also have a strong desire to make the *effort* necessary to fulfill a goal. The desire to reach the goal and the desire to make the effort are not the same. We will soon see why this distinction is so important.

The strong desire to fulfill a goal is the spark that starts the motivational fire. The strong desire to make the effort is what keeps the fire burning. This desire is more in the form of *willing* than trying. It is deciding to push on rather than trying to keep going. This is discipline! It is a commitment to yourself. The type of goals that elite athletes set demands that a continuing, sustained effort be made. In the case of super-athletes, we are talking about a period of, perhaps, 20 or more years. This explains, in part, why some athletes, such as **Wade Boggs**, **Wayne Gretzky**, and **Tiger Woods** are such incredible athletes. They all started to play their game as children. The motivational fires must continue to burn if one is to produce high-quality performances over a prolonged period of time. It is the desire to make the sustained effort that keeps the fire burning.

The third part of our definition deals with the *goals* that super-athletes work to achieve. The kinds of goals that super-athletes set allow them to feel confident in their ability to be successful. Success then builds on success—further fueling the fire and producing even more confidence in the athlete. Remember, the motivational fires must continue to burn if an athlete is to produce high-quality performances over a prolonged period of time. Without success, the fire could easily go out.

In addition to the strength of an athlete's desire, motivation is affected by the athlete's expectations of success. In particular, athletes' beliefs that they *know how* to fulfill their goals and their beliefs that they have the *ability* to fulfill their goals are extremely important. If athletes don't believe they know how to do what is necessary or don't believe that they have the physical or mental ability necessary, their motivation can decrease, or even disappear. Without exception, super-athletes are certain they know how to do what has to be done. They are almost resolute in their beliefs that they have the ability to successfully carry out what has to be done.

In summary, there are three major parts to our definition of motivation. First, there is the strength of the person's *desire*. Second, there is the *effort* necessary to fulfill a goal. Third, there is the particular *goal* that the person is trying to complete. So, as you can see, motivation is a complex phenomenon. For motivation to be at its highest, these elements must be fulfilled in an optimal way.

BIG GOALS

For an athlete the Big Goal can generally be defined as the "reason I play the game." That sounds simple enough, right? When we interview athletes during the NBA draft, they often tell us, "I play because I love the game." But when we ask them, "What do you mean by 'love the game?'" they give a wide variety of answers. For some it is "an opportunity to get rich." For some it is "I want to be famous." For others it is "an opportunity to take care of my family." For yet others it is "a place for me to find refuge." So, on the surface these players all appeared to have the same Big Goal—love of the game. Yet, when we looked at their Big Goals more closely, it became clear that each had very different goals. They played the game to fulfill their own fundamental needs. To fully understand Big Goals, we have to question the deeper meanings they hold for the athlete.

How about you? Why do you do what you do? What is your Big Goal? Take a moment and think about it. Have you ever really looked closely at your actions and tried to be honest with yourself? Have you ever truly analyzed your motivations? After all, your Big Goal is the fuel for your actions. For better or worse, it is what propels you through life.

Let's look at an example. One athlete we interviewed said that his Big Goal was "to provide for his family." Fine, that is one level of meaning. But, let's probe deeper. We asked the athlete, "If you provide for your family, what will that mean to you?"

His response was, "It means I will be taking care of what is important to me."

"Which is?" we asked.

He replied, "Not feeling alone and knowing that I will always be around people who accept me for who I am. I will feel that I have done my job. I will feel competent in their eyes and in mine. I don't have to prove myself anymore."

The Big Goal for this athlete was being unconditionally accepted by others in order to feel competent about himself. Do you see how a single Big Goal can have many layers of meaning? The Big Goal was initially "providing for family." After much discussion and thought, this athlete came to realize that his Big Goal was "feeling competent." Not all people or super-athletes are driven by the need to feel competent. There are other Big Goals. However, as we shall see, super-athletes seem to share a unique way of meeting their needs. They have a way of fulfilling their Big Goals that allows them to be more successful than others.

It is not easy for a person to change or manipulate a Big Goal at the deepest levels. In fact, we have found it to be nearly impossible. In our practice and research we have discovered these need to be a natural part of a person's psychological profile. It isn't as if at some point people make a conscious decision to have a particular need; rather, the need is a fundamental part of a person's make-up. It may even have a genetic component. It is, regardless of origin, how we see ourselves. We view these Big Goals as ways to complete ourselves and fulfill what demands fulfillment. They allow us to realize the potential we all have locked within ourselves. Because they are part of our make-up, they are always present. This helps explain the super-athletes' "hunger"—why they seem not quite ever to be satisfied with their accomplishments. Just as a big meal soon gives way to the feeling of hunger again, the Big Goals keep appearing and driving them to once again attempt to reach their objective—to fulfill that potential which demands expression.

The Big Goal is the super-athlete's primary source of motivation. That much we know. But, what does this motivation look like? Are super-athletes driven in a unique way? Do they simply have greater talent and desire or is it also the type of goal that contributes to their remarkable performances? Stated simply, why do they play the game? To help us answer these questions, let's turn to the super-athletes themselves and see what they say.

WHAT THE SUPER-ATHLETES SAY

Motivation is crucial—in sports and life. Some athletes are not only more talented than others are, they are also more driven. But why? What lights the competitive fire of the super-athlete? What gets them going and, just as important, what keeps them going?

The first step in understanding the motivation of the super-athlete is to look at what we call their Big Goals. Ask yourself the following questions:

What is really important to you? What are your most important values? What drives you? In short—Why do you do what you do? Notice that we can now be talking about a person's essential goals: What it is that is at the root of the person's personality? What it is that drives the person through life?

Big Goals are actually *fundamental needs*, a part of the super-athletes' personal philosophies—something they must fulfill if they are to feel whole. These fundamental needs have two sides: a strong desire to fulfill them as well as a strong fear of not fulfilling them. This combination of desire and fear brings passion and intensity to their actions.

Big Goals are obviously important, essential, what really matters, what the super-athlete is really striving for. Little Goals are how they reach their Big Goals. For example, a person may have a Big Goal of being a good father. Working hard at his job and spending quality time with his children might be Little Goals that would help him reach his Big Goal. In tennis, a player might have a Big Goal of being a top player. A Little Goal might be to develop a reliable second serve. Little Goals are typically more specific and concrete than Big Goals. Big Goals are more permanent and stable—they reflect our personal makeup. Big Goals are more often *out of our control*, while Little Goals are much *easier to control*, but both Big Goals and Little Goals are extremely important in enhancing motivation. Let's see how the super-athletes see it.[1]

JACK NICKLAUS (Golf)

Immersed in Challenge

Surprisingly, golf has never been an obsession for **Jack Nicklaus**. Instead, it's part of a bigger picture. "Nothing consumes me," he said. "I live a life of balance. I want to win at everything I do, and I try to give everything. I give my best effort. But if having done so, and I lose, then so be it. Life goes on. Golf is just a game. There will many more days of golf and there are a million other interesting things to do in life."

Why, then, does Jack play the game? "I love golf," he said. "Money and applause have only been incidental. What is important is the *challenge* of the game. Golf really excites me when the course is difficult and challenging."

For Jack, simply being part of the competition—having an opportunity to be successful—is what really matters. As he put it, "It is doing one's best for its own sake." Competition, in business as well as sports, energizes Jack. It keeps him young and enthusiastic. There is intensity during those pressurized moments of competition that puts him in touch with something primal. "It makes me feel alive," he said. "Life is intensified."

So what, precisely was Jack's Big Goal? Having the opportunity to be challenged and to compete. As is so often the case with the super-athlete, though, his emphasis was on the *process*, rather than on the *result*; on the *playing*, rather than on the *outcome*.

MICHAEL JORDAN (Basketball)

Intensity of Competition

Michael Jordan, of course, is considered by many to be the greatest basketball player in history. The game seemed effortless to him; in truth, though, he was one of the most competitive athletes to ever have played any sport.

"A lot of people play like it is only a game," he said. "Not me! I love to compete. I like the *challenge*. If I'm going to play, then I'm going to play to win. That is enjoyable to me. That's fun!"

Michael was never satisfied. Even in practice, he worked as hard as he possibly could. Each scrimmage was played with an intense desire to outplay his "opponent" (teammate). This does not, however, mean that Michael was selfish. Although he was one of the most prolific scorers in NBA history and the type of player who always liked to take the last game-winning or game-losing shot—in short, a great one-on-one player—Michael was most driven by team goals. "Just give me more championship rings," he said. For him, team goals were personal goals.

Once again, though, the result is not the focus. The journey or process is what really matters. Michael loved basketball. As he pointed out, "I can always go and talk to the game. It is a place of refuge." More than anything, basketball gave Michael an opportunity to compete, to challenge himself. As much as he wanted to win, he knew that victory was meaningless without effort. "It doesn't matter if I win as long as I give everything in my heart and work at it 110%," he said. "I can accept failure. Everyone fails at something. But I cannot accept not trying." Notice the subtle difference here. It's very important. Michael's goal was to make the decision to try to win—to make the effort. It was not necessarily winning. It was to do all he could to win. That was his challenge.[2]

Can you see the Big Goal here? For Michael, it was this: becoming the best through meeting challenge after challenge. Even though there is a clear and reachable goal at the end, the focus is on climbing from one level to the next. Winning is obviously important, but it is the *challenge* and *effort* that matter most. The challenge may have been going head-to-head against the other team's best defensive player; it might have been related to being a "marked man" in every game he played; or it might have been being physically roughed up and still being able to overcome. It may have been to make his teammates better and more a part of the game; it certainly included the challenge of winning the next NBA Championship and putting forth the effort needed to make that happen.

JOAN BENOIT (Track)

Competing for Acceptance

Joan Benoit is widely regarded as the one of the greatest female distance runners in U.S. history. Her inner strength and competitive zeal helped her win the Olympic Gold in the marathon and become a world record holder, despite a series of painful and debilitating injuries. What fueled that competitive fire? For Joan, it was always the challenge. "I had two brothers when I was growing up," she said. "I had to learn to compete."

Distance running was not popular in Joan's native Maine, yet she felt compelled to pursue the sport. Her motivation came from within. She said:

> I sometimes even felt embarrassed to run, but nothing could keep me from it. I loved the internal *challenge*. I set internal goals. I wanted to push myself to see what I could do. Some of my goals included fear; others did not. But I felt the only way to fail was not to try. I believe that God expects me to push against all obstacles with all my strength and give up only when I am fairly and honestly defeated.

For Joan, as we so often see with other super-athletes, it is the challenge—the quest—that motivates. The final step of one journey is merely the first step of another. "For as long as I can remember, I've been setting goals for myself and dealing with the consequences of either meeting or failing them."

WAYNE GRETZKY (Hockey)

Proving his Natural Talents to Doubters

There is a reason that Wayne Gretzky is known as "The Great One." No one has ever played hockey with such grace and style. So often he has reminded us that hockey is not merely a game of muscle and mayhem; it is also a game of speed and beauty … of artistry.

In fact, it was the game itself that motivated Wayne—the opportunity to explore and utilize his talents. The cups and trophies and money were nice, but they were merely rewards for achieving his Big Goal. "There is more to this game than myself," said Wayne. "They ought to call me 'the Grateful One.' I have worked hard—as hard as anybody. But you don't have to tell me a lot of my talent is God-given. I know that."

Wayne's humility was reflected in his approach to the sport. While he is proud of having the NHL's MVP award, it is the team accomplishments he remembers the most. He took as much pleasure in assisting on a goal as he did in scoring one himself. Hard to believe? Well, consider this: When Wayne broke the NHL record for most goals in a season, he forgot to retrieve the historic puck!

Overall, Wayne focused on the game and the *challenges* it presented to himself and his team. The Big Goal for him was achievement. "I always thought there was no use shooting for a medium goal," he said. "You have to shoot for the highest goal. I had a lot to prove. There were always a few doubters."

MARIO ANDRETTI (Auto Racing)

Taking Risks as a Challenge

Mario Andretti was one of the most successful drivers in the history of auto racing. As is often the case with super-athletes, he was quite young—only about 10 years old—when he first became enthralled by the sport that would make him famous. Mario told us:

> I didn't want to do anything else in life but race. I used to get goose bumps watching the races on sports highlights. Living in Italy, there was lots of national pride—the Italian Grand Prix, Ferraris, etc. There was a whole slew of frontline drivers in the fifties. Racing was the thing. I had only one sight all the way through high school, and that was to be a driver. I didn't care about having my own car or racing team. My whole objective was to find a way to get noticed so that I could move on.

For Mario, the Big Goal in racing was the challenge. He loved to set goals and continuously achieve. "I don't want to get hurt, but life without risk is too mundane," he said. "There needs to be the *challenge*. I have to have something to gain or lose. If there's no challenge, there's nothing to gain and the mind retires and motivation leaves. The challenge was to make this beast [car] work really hard and not let it bite me."

RAY NITSCHKE (Football)

Drive for Perfection

Hall of Fame linebacker **Ray Nitschke** anchored the defense for the Green Bay Packer teams of the 1960s. Fiercely competitive and aggressive, he was a favorite of Coach Vince Lombardi, from whom he learned a thing or two about motivation.

"Football was my passion," Ray said. "I was completely committed—to practice, to the game—I'd take it home with me—played with reckless abandon, like there was no tomorrow. I competed against myself. I was always driving for perfection, never getting there. I was never satisfied. There was no ceiling."

Ray said a number of things motivated him: "I wanted to be recognized, respected for what I could do. Even more important, I wanted to win. I expected us to win. There was never a doubt about winning. If we lost, I'd just learn from it, let go of it, turn my attention to the next game."

Like Lombardi, Ray Nitschke never allowed himself to become comfortable with what he had achieved. Although, realistically unattainable, Ray's Big Goal and challenge was perfection. Whether in practice or a game, each play—each moment—was the most important of his career. And every Sunday was Super Bowl Sunday!

WADE BOGGS (Baseball)

Self-Identity as Winner

Wade Boggs was one of baseball's greatest contact hitters. He is a "throwback" to the old days of the sport when playing injured was commonplace. His love of the game was clearly demonstrated by his reluctance to come out of the lineup and his passion for studying the game and working to improve. He said, "I love the game. I started playing little league when I was five years old. I have always loved the game. It has been a part of my life. It is something I have always done." What was behind this love of the game for Wade?

What was really important to me was the competition—the *challenge*, the pressures, all of that. I always anticipated winning. I never had the thought that we were going to get beat today. I expected to win. And if we didn't, it was the bad part of the day but I could let it go because I knew we were not going to win them all. If we won 90 games, then we could be in the playoffs.

JIM RYUN (Track)

Recognition for Excellence

Jim Ryun was arguably one of America's greatest distance runners and its most famous miler. A tall, skinny kid from the Kansas farmlands, he took the world by storm while still in high school. Listen as he talks about his development as a runner:

> Initially, I wanted to be part of an athletic team to get a letter and a girl-friend. Later my goals became people and times. People were competition and time was the *challenge*. We did a tremendous amount of work as preparation. I quickly went from racing against individuals to racing against the clock. Coach Timmons planted the seed that I could be the first high-school four-minute miler. I started to believe what Coach was saying. It wasn't just being the best miler; it was running under four minutes. The next step was the U.S. Olympic team and the next, the world record. We just kept pushing barriers back. We didn't want to place limits on what I could do.

We asked Jim to tell us more about what he meant about limits. He went on, "Limits would come in terms of how I would think, train, or the amount of physical work that I could handle. This had more to do with limits within myself, my abilities."

RICHARD PETTY (Auto Racing)

Life Immersion

Richard Petty, known as "The King" and the all-time NASCAR win leader, talked about where his motivation came from. "I was around racing since I was 10 years old. My whole life was built around racing. I maybe didn't retire when I should have but my love for racing was so great that I couldn't turn my back on it. The love was just the feel of racing—the competition, the *challenges*."

Richard described his goal:

> Why did I race? I had a burning desire to compete and when I competed, I felt I could do as good as anybody on that particular day. Racing was an

inner need that I developed over a period of years and basically when it gets right down to it—it was my life. When we first got married I told my wife, "Racing is number one, and if you try real hard you can be number two." This kept my focus. I breathed racing 24 hours a day.

For Richard, his intensity goes all the way back to childhood. "I always wanted to win, I never thought about being the best. But if I didn't win, it wasn't the end of the world because we will have another race, another challenge next week. I did a lot of my career on self-satisfaction, just staying within myself."

Richard went on, "I am a big believer in fate. I try to control only those things that I can. Whether bad breaks or good breaks came, I tried to take advantage of them. I tried to do the best I could with whatever the situation was."

Doug Rogers (Judo)

Level the Playing Field

Doug Rogers was the first Caucasian to compete in the Japanese National Judo Championships. He won a Silver Medal in the heavyweight category at the 1964 Tokyo Olympics, the Bronze Medal at the World Judo Championships in Rio de Janeiro, and a Gold Medal at the Pan American Judo Championships in Guatemala the following year.

The son of a clergyman, Doug was often the brunt of bullies in part because of his quiet nature. Doug was determined to stand up for himself.

I was intrigued by the apparent ease with which experts could overcome opponents even though disadvantaged in size and strength. When we moved to Ontario, I exhausted the very limited supply of information on jujitsu and judo that existed in the public library. I would often stand in front of my bedroom mirror and try to copy the moves as best I could or sometimes I would get my Dad to wrestle with me on the living room floor. Occasionally, I persuaded a friend to be my partner. I think I can safely say I am the only person to have thrown the famed Chicago Blackhawks' Stan Mikita in a foot sweep. Stan was a good friend—we played together on an Ontario hockey champion team.

Doug's primitive learning of judo before he got into training helped him survive. "On a few occasions my crude understanding of a few holds helped me level the playing field when bigger boys tried to pick on me."

3

HOW CHALLENGES MOTIVATE THE SUPER-ATHLETE

Super-athletes fulfill their essential needs through meeting challenges. Meeting challenges is their Big Goal. As you can see, even among super-athletes, some goals are more common than others are. The super-athletes will often say that what they enjoy most about their sports is the competition, the journey. For this type of athlete, the greatest satisfaction comes not only from winning the game, but also from successfully meeting the challenges of the game. Every game and every sport has its own challenges—such as facing the best pitcher on another team, playing against the best team in the league, playing through fatigue, playing with an injury, playing in front of a hostile crowd, having to play under very adverse weather conditions, playing in an important game when key teammates are injured—the list goes on. Super-athletes face these kinds of challenges on a day-to-day basis. They also face long-term challenges, such as trying to be the best, trying to master their sport, or even, for some, discovering what their limits are. The awards, money, victories, and fame—they are all nice. It's rare, though, to find a super-athlete who considers any of those things to be a Big Goal. Challenge is the Big Goal for super-athletes.

As we saw earlier, there can be deeper meanings to motivation. The same is true of challenge. Although super-athletes often stated it as a Big Goal, upon closer inspection we found that challenge meant different things to different super-athletes. In fact, it can mean several things to the same athlete. Suppose an athlete says, "I love the challenge of my sport." What does that statement mean? The athlete could be referring to the challenge of becoming an expert at what needs to be done. This is *mastery*. It could also refer to the challenge of wanting to accomplish as much as possible or more than anybody else does. This is *achievement*. Finally, it could refer to the challenge of finding out exactly what the person is capable of doing—psychologically, as well as physically. This is *competence*. Let's take a closer look at these three faces of challenge.

MASTERY

START AT AN EARLY AGE

One type of challenge that super-athletes try to meet is mastery. By overcoming day-to-day challenges they move toward the elusive goal of self-perfection. The super-athletes who seek mastery are trying to be the very best they can be at what they do. They want to perfect their craft: gain as much knowledge as possible, perform flawlessly and effortlessly, in short, become as skilled as they can possibly be.

Ted Williams was a classic example of an athlete in pursuit of mastery. He learned everything he could about the details of hitting. He studied opposing pitchers. He studied the mechanics of hitting. He developed his own philosophy of hitting. Ted was single-minded in his drive to master the art of hitting a baseball.

Hall of Fame quarterback, Johnny Unitas of the Baltimore Colts, had trouble getting into college because his grades were not high, yet he became a true student of football. He studied film for hours on end, until he knew everything there was to know about his opponent. Interestingly, by the time he retired, Johnny was considered one of the smartest quarterbacks to ever play in the NFL.

Similarly, **Jerry Rice** of the San Francisco 49ers was legendary in his pursuit of perfection. From grueling off-season workouts to an intense pre-game ritual in which he could usually be found running pass patterns all alone, over and over, Jerry's focus was always on mastery. In pursuit of his perfection, Jerry worked as hard as any player in the league, and, of course, he got results. That combination prompted other players to fear and respect Jerry, which he liked. This was one way he knew he was achieving mastery.

Judo champion Doug Rogers' interest in judo started at a young age, while reading the back of comic books. "I started judo when I was 15, living in Montreal," he told us, "but my interest had been kindled years earlier when as a youngster I read about the mysterious arts of self-defense called 'jujitsu' and 'combat judo,' often featured on the back cover advertisements of comic books."

For each of these athletes, challenge can best be defined as mastery. Take a moment and think about how long it might take to master a particular sport. This is clearly a long-term proposition. Skills need to be learned, practiced, and perfected. Mental strategies need to be developed. Athletes need to learn how to deal effectively with both success and failure. This all takes time. That is precisely why the long-term side of motivation is so important. Not only does the motivational fire have to burn, it must continue to burn for a long time. If athletes get discouraged early in their careers, they may come to doubt they have "the right stuff" (ability), and their motivation can diminish. This makes it more unlikely they will experience success in the future and hampers their chances of long-term success.

ACHIEVEMENT

GROOM SUCCESS AT SUCCESSIVE LEVELS

Challenge can mean achievement—large and small. For instance, each time you meet a challenge, you've not only reached a specific goal, you have also taken a step toward some larger goal. With achievement, the goal is not necessarily being the best you can be, but continuously striving for improvement. For super-athletes who equate challenge with achievement, satisfaction is elusive. Instead of seeking a particular result, super-athletes seek to collect as many positive results as they can. They always believe they can do better or accomplish more.

Dallas Cowboy running back, **Emmitt Smith**, collected footballs from every game he played and recorded his accomplishments on each. **Jeff Bagwell** of the Houston Astros, one of baseball's top players, said, "I am never satisfied. I am always reaching for the next level. The MVP award was nice, but winning a World Series is next."

For the super-athlete, a key to success is the ability to move from one level to the next, to stay hungry, regardless of how full his belly appears to be. **Gordie Howe**, the standard against whom many hockey players measure their achievements, said his big goal was "to play forever and break the record for longevity." True to his word, Gordie, at the age of 69, became the first player to play professional hockey in six different decades.

Deion Sanders, the two-sport star for the Dallas Cowboys and the Cincinnati Reds, offered a slightly different twist to achievement. "I want to be the best and take things to a new level—to do the undone, to show the unseen, to be creative. I want to do what has never been done before." For Deion, challenge equaled achievement, but it also meant innovation.

Judo champion, Doug Rogers, was inspired to move ahead by what he saw at higher levels. "When I was 17, I won the Eastern Canadian non-black belt title. At that same tournament I was struck by the great skill of the black belt champion who had trained in Japan. He defeated his opponents with little difficulty. I became determined to go to Japan."

COMPETENCE

EXCEL WITHIN YOUR OWN KNOWN LIMITS

Challenge can mean competence—an opportunity to prove to yourself that you can do something. The focus is on the process: the "can do"—rather than the results: the "have done." Champion golfer, **Gary Player**, told us he wanted to feel competent so that he could accept whatever obstacles the game presented. Hall of Fame quarterback, **Y. A. Tittle** said, "I just wanted to play. Football was part of me. I loved the competition. My goal was always to just jump in there. I knew what I could do. That was my focus. I was fearless."

All Star **Craig Biggio** said, "I love all aspects of the game—fielding hitting, everything. My goal is to stay consistent and even. So, if I go zero for four at bat, I can still make a great fielding play and feel good about the game." Craig knows better than to put all of his eggs in one basket. For him, the challenge is to feel competent about doing many things well.

Competence is a challenge that many super-athletes appear to accept. They all seem to have gained a clear idea of what they can do—what their abilities are and the limits of those abilities. In fact, one of the characteristics that sets super-athletes apart from "ordinary" athletes is their willingness to "play within their limits" while, at the same time, "set no limits."

Think about this for a moment. It sounds contradictory at first, doesn't it? Stay within limits yet set no limits? How can someone do that? Well, let's take Deion Sanders as an example. Deion had a clear idea of what his strengths and weaknesses were. He had proven to himself what he could do in athletics (in the physical sense). For example, he knew that he would never be a home run hitter on the order of Mark McGuire. For him to try and hit 40 home runs a year would be playing outside of his limits. At the same time, Deion knew his speed and his base running abilities. So, he might set out to perfect the art of base running (mastery). He might try to steal more bases than anyone else had in Cincinnati history (achievement). What is clear from interviews with Deion is that he did not want to set any limits on what he might accomplish as long as he played within his perceived limits. He wanted to "show the unseen … do the undone." He wanted to "be creative." He did just this when he played both offense and defense and returned kicks for the Dallas Cowboys. While staying within his limits, he tried to be the most entertaining player he could be. Along with many other super-athletes, the important thing for Deion was to understand the limits of his abilities and continue to push to the next level within these limits. In short, they strive to be unlimited within the limits of their abilities.

RESPECT

ENJOY SUCCEEDING IN THE MOMENT

Coaches often go out of their way to say something flattering about an opponent. Sometimes it borders on the humorous. "So and So University is very deceptive. I know they have won only three games in the past 4 years, but they are the best 0-and-8 team in the country!" Why do they do this? The answer is simple. Almost everyone wants respect. It is one of the strongest human needs. Coaches do not want opponents to believe they are not respected. They know how strong the need for respect is. Players, it seems, are not always so careful. In the heat of the moment, they can make inflammatory statements that wind up on an opponent's locker-room wall. Few things motivate a team or player more than apparent lack of respect from an opponent.

Interestingly enough, although important, getting respect does not appear to be the major issue with most super-athletes; rather, their goals are focused on the mastery, the achievements or developing the competence that will lead to respect. Respect is something that just about everybody likes, but it does not represent a specific "inner" goal like the challenges of mastery, achievement, and competence. Rather it is focused "outside" the athlete and on the responses of others. As Ted Williams once said, "All I want is for people to say, 'There goes the greatest hitter who ever played the game.'" When getting respect does become an issue, it is most often put in the form of a challenge. We have heard many super-athletes echo the sentiments of Olympic sprinting champion and world record holder **Michael Johnson:** "I just love it when someone says I can't do something. That really gets me going." It is clear that getting respect was a challenge that was important to Michael Johnson.

Challenge is not an important motivator for many athletes, particularly for "ordinary" athletes. In any athletic competition there is the process (the playing of the game) and the result (the outcome, which determines success or failure for many). Challenge, generally speaking, is part of the process.

Super-athletes see it as an obstacle or resistance that must be overcome if one is to be successful. Their day-to-day goals help them overcome this resistance and the obstacles they encounter while trying to meet their Big Goals.

Instead of focusing on a process such as overcoming an obstacle, most ordinary athletes only consider results as important. Ted Williams once told us that as a youngster he focused too heavily on results: "At first, I played the game for pride. I just wanted to know I could do it as good as anybody. Challenge came later, when I got results and knew what I could do."

Then, of course, there is the flip side, the more playful attitude: Don't worry about winning. Just have fun! In this case, the process—the playing of the game—is the focus. Results matter less.

We will give you an example that illustrates these options. Each student in a sport psychology class was assigned the task of tossing a tennis ball into a large basket. They could choose to stand at any distance from the basket. Some of the students chose to throw the ball from the back of the room—a nearly impossible distance. They laughed and acted playful toward the task. For these students the goal was unrealistic; therefore, there was no challenge and nothing to lose.

Other students walked right up to the basket and dropped the ball in. They, too, were interested in something other than a real challenge; they were only interested in obtaining a positive outcome. Finally, there were those few that chose to shoot from an intermediate distance. These were the students most motivated by challenge. Not surprisingly, no one chose the short distance that was perceived as easy but where failure was still a possibility.

Obviously, some of the students were more interested in challenge than others. The same is true with athletes. The challenging Big Goals of super-athletes can be quite different from the goals of ordinary athletes. Notably absent among super-athletes are Big Goals such as …

- I need to be liked
- I want to look good
- I need to avoid losing self-worth
- I want to feel good and have fun

Make no mistake—super-athletes often value such things; however, because they are much more secure than the average athlete (or the average person for that matter), their Big Goals are usually linked to challenge. Challenge is the spark that lights the flame, and the type of challenge can be the desire for mastery, achievement, or competence.

LITTLE GOALS: THE AIM IN COMPETITION

We've looked at the Big Goals of super-athletes. Now let's look at their Little Goals—that is, their *competition goals*. These are the goals they use in the heat of battle. Smaller, focused, and invaluable, competition goals are used by a batter waiting for a pitch, a quarterback about to take the snap from center, a point guard bringing the ball up court, a golfer lining up a putt, or a tennis player preparing to serve. In addition to these examples, which reflect the setting of goals during the flow of a contest, competition goals can be set immediately before a game, or even during a break. Super-athletes seem to know, almost instinctively, how to set effective competition goals and how to avoid the pitfalls of goals that undermine successful performance.

SUPER-ATHLETES IN THE HEAT OF COMPETITION

What type of competition goals do super-athletes set? Can these goals give us some insight into their extraordinary performances? We believe they can. It might surprise you to learn that obvious competition goals like hitting a home run, scoring a touchdown, or sinking the putt are not typical competition goals for super-athletes. The super-athlete sets even smaller and more precise competition goals. These "Little Goals" are ones that super-athletes feel confident they can achieve. They see these goals as controllable and attainable.

Let's take a look.

BASEBALL

"Attack the ball and don't let the ball attack me."—**Hank Aaron**

"Stand in the same place in the batter's box every time."—**Ted Williams**

"Swing where the ball is pitched."—**Willie Mays**

"Swing as hard as I can and try to swing right through the ball."—**Babe Ruth**

"Get the barrel on the ball and make contact."—**Tony Gwynn**

"... swing right through the ball."

"Take what the pitcher is giving me and adjust."—**Craig Biggio**

"Try to hit the ball hard."—**Alan Trammel**

"Hit the ball squarely."—**Barry Larkin**

"Be a predator—pounce on the prey (ball) and hit it hard."—**Matt Williams**

"See the ball and give myself a chance to get a base hit."—**Hal McRae**

"Bring in base runners."—**Cecil Fielder**

"Hit the ball hard."—**Hal McRae**

FOOTBALL

"I want the ball so I can do something with it."—**Joe Montana**

"Be wild and run to wherever the ball is."—**Lawrence Taylor**

"Act like a warrior, like Superman, for my teammates."—**Jim Brown**

"Act like a warrior ... for my teammates."

"I want to win and play my best in every game I play."—**Joe Namath**

"Score as much as possible and take as much as I can get."—**Johnny Unitas**

"Stay in the game and don't have anyone take my place."—**Y. A. Tittle**

"To contribute as much as I can."—**Ray Nitschke**

BASKETBALL

"Be willing to take what the defense gives me."—**Michael Jordan**

"Go all out and make sure I never play bad."—**Larry Bird**

"Go full tilt with an explosive and reckless disregard for whoever or whatever stands in my way."—**Charles Barkley**

"I never know what is enough, so go full throttle."—**Isiah Thomas**

"... go full throttle."

"Focus on the game situation and us winning."—**Jerry West**

GOLF

"Attack the course rather than play it cautiously."—**Arnold Palmer**

"Give it my best effort and go for the win."—**Jack Nicklaus**

"Do my best and accept adversity."—**Gary Player**

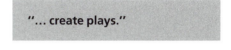
"Attack the course."

HOCKEY

"Score goals and create plays."—**Wayne Gretzky**

"Score one goal every third game."—**Gordie Howe**

"... create plays."

BOXING

"Act like a warrior who is obliged to carry on through thick and thin."—**Joe Frazier**

"Act like a warrior."

TRACK

"Ignore time and run as fast as I can from start to finish."—**Joan Benoit**

"Ignore time."

AUTO RACING

"Always be on a mission, striving to the next level."—**Mario Andretti**

"Be present and react to whatever is happening"—**Richard Petty**

"Be present ..."

TENNIS

"Never lose eye contact; never wonder where the ball is going."—**Chris Evert**

"Never lose eye contact ..."

Can you see how these Little Goals are, for the most part, more under the control of the super-athlete? Can you see why they feel confident they can achieve these Little Goals? If achieved, these *Little Goals* help the super-athlete achieve their *Big Goals, meeting challenges*. Notice how simple these competition goals are in most cases. "I focus on the little things. Little things add up to big things," said Michael Jordan. "I'm still going to get up and work out in the morning, and do the necessary things. If you have something else you want to do, fine. I'll catch up with you. But I am not going to be talked into looking the other way."[1] The super-athlete may well be striving to demonstrate competence or to achieve mastery or to accumulate additional achievements. However, these Big Goals are in the background. The direct object of the super-athlete's concentration during the moment of competition is the Little Goals, the competition goals that can lead to successfully meeting the Big Goal of challenge, through *mastery, achievement,* or *competence*.

Look at the Little Goals listed above. Perhaps you can see that there are other ways of thinking about them, in addition to classifying them as Little Goals or competition goals. Some of the goals are focused on what we call the *process*, what is going on moment-to-moment in a contest. Others are focused on *results* like the final outcome. Moreover, some are *avoidance goals* in which fear is the primary motivation. The athlete is trying to avoid some negative outcome. Others are *approach goals*, in which desire is the primary motivation. The athlete is trying to reach (approach) some desired end state. Let's take a closer look at these different ways of classifying Little Goals and see how they relate to the motivation of the super-athlete.

5

RESULTS AND PROCESS

Ask yourself this simple question: do you live in the moment or are you constantly looking ahead? Your answer to that simple question will go a long way toward determining the types of goals you set. This is true regardless of whether we are talking about a competitive situation or a day-to-day life situation. Let's consider competition.

What are the main components of a competitive situation? To begin with, of course, there are the participants (you and your opponents). Next is the game itself—the event, and within the game are specific objectives and goals. Such goals can, and often do, refer to outcomes such as winning and losing. They also refer to the steps required to produce a desired outcome, such as winning. Don't confuse these goals, though. They are intertwined and closely connected, but clearly separate. Don't believe it? Try to think of both goals—for example, swinging a golf club well … and … winning—at precisely the same time. It can't be done. You can't simultaneously think about what you must do in order to win and think about winning. You can do one or the other, but not both.

It is, however, possible to think of one goal (swinging the club well) and then quickly think of the other (winning). So, we have two different types of goals that may be involved in any given competition. *Result goals* refer to a particular outcome in a game (like winning or scoring a touchdown or getting a hit). *Process* refers to performance goals and includes the steps a person can take to achieve the result goals. Performance goals may be things like "watch my blockers," which could lead to a touchdown, or "put the barrel of the bat on the ball," which could lead to getting a base hit.

Notice that performance goals are *more specific and concrete*. Because of this, athletes can have more control over performance goals than they can over result goals. A baseball player can take a perfect swing and hit a line drive, and a fielder might make a lucky catch. Everything was perfect, except the player didn't get a hit. Was the hitter successful? It depends upon the goal, doesn't it? If the goal was to hit the ball hard or to take a good swing, the hitter was successful. If the goal was only to get a base hit, then the hitter failed.

Now that you have an idea of the differences between result goals and performance goals, let's take a closer look at how super-athletes use them.

RESULT GOALS

Result goals, while widely regarded as necessary for success, can also cause problems. Consider football. One example of a result goal is "score a touchdown." Another is "win the game." In baseball a result goal might be "hit a home run." In boxing a common result goal is "knock out the opponent." On the surface these sound fine. They show a desire to achieve positive results. The problem is that athletes often focus too heavily on these "frozen" images of what they want to occur at the end of an action. If athletes are too busy envisioning victory or some other result goal, they are less able to concentrate on taking the steps necessary to achieve the desired goal. We have all seen what can happen to a wide receiver who is already thinking about celebrating in the end zone before he reaches the goal line!

Goals that focus too strongly on outcomes can be dangerous. In fact, if not channeled properly, they can actually undermine your efforts to be successful. Listen to what All-Pro and Hall of Fame linebacker **Steve Kiner** said on this subject:

> When I have a result goal, I'm thinking ahead. I am not in the process of moment-to-moment action. When I am not in the moment, it's like everything is on fast-forward. There is no flow or continuity, only discrete changes. In this state, I can get surprised; things can sneak up on me. But when I am in the process and in the flow, I feel like I am a part of everything. It's like a dance.[1]

Kiner's point is well taken. Suppose you're playing a game. What's your goal? To win? To beat your opponent? To do your best? To watch your opponent and make the right decision? To go for the win? The differences here are obvious: the first two goals refer to outcomes (result goals). In each case you are focusing on how you want things to turn out. You are not giving your full attention to the task at hand—the process. Instead you are concerned with the outcome. In some ways the game is going on without you! These are result goals. The next three goals are performance goals. They reflect what might be going on in a game or competition. They also are much more under the control of an athlete than winning or beating one's opponent.

But wait! Consider the first and last goals. "Wanting to win" and "going for the win" are not at all the same. With "wanting to win," your focus is far up ahead, at the end of the contest. You just want to get there. The journey means nothing. When you add, "go for it," "shoot for it," or "try" to your goal, however, the meaning changes. Now you are not only focusing on the result but also on the process you need to get the result. Effort becomes an important part of the equation. Your focus is now on the moment-to-moment activities needed to win or beat an opponent. The difference is subtle but critical. Winning is seldom under an athlete's control. Trying or going for the win is always something an athlete can control. Can you see the difference?

We have talked to many super-athletes who say their primary competition goal is "to play hard and win." Rarely do they say their goal is simply to win. Effort, to the super-athlete, is imperative. The process of playing hard leads to the desired result—winning. There are no short cuts. Result goals, then, can be of two types: those that incorporate process and those that focus exclusively on outcome. Super-athletes usually choose the former.

PERFORMANCE GOALS

In the example above, the performance goals are "to do your best," "to watch your opponent and make the right decision," and "to go for the win." In these cases, the athlete's focus is on *the effort necessary to reach the goal*, rather than just on the end goal. The athlete is in the moment.

How do super-athletes speak of performance goals? Michael Jordan put it this way: "I would wake up in the morning thinking, 'OK, how am I going to attack today?'" Joe Namath said, "I want to win and play my best in every game I play." Jack Nicklaus tried to "give my best effort and go for the win." Larry Bird's focus was on "… going all out and make sure I never play bad." Interesting, isn't it? Although super-athletes emphasize the processes involved in competition, they do so in the context of results. We have not found a single case of a super-athlete whose goal is simply "to do my best."

Some super-athletes have highly imaginative performance goals. World heavyweight boxing champion, Joe Frazier, for example, wanted "to act like a warrior who is obliged to carry on through thick and thin." All-time great running back, Jim Brown, focused on "acting like a warrior, like Superman." These are performance goals that require a type of role playing. They are, however, like other performance goals, just a means to an end. The role is adopted so that a desired outcome can be achieved. The focus is on the process.

Perhaps the most common type of performance goal occurs during the flow of the action in a contest and is focused on a momentary target. For Michael Jordan, the performance goal was "taking what the defense gives me." Others, such as Ted Williams, Barry Larkin, Tony Gwynn, and Matt Williams, focused on getting a good pitch to hit, getting the bat on the ball, or even, simply, standing in the same place in the batter's box every time. For Lawrence Taylor, perhaps the greatest linebacker of all time, the performance goal was "be wild and run to wherever the ball is."

For all these athletes, performance goals include targets found within the actual space of the game situation—and the targets lead to results. In all of our extensive research, we found pure performance goals—those that are completely unrelated to results—to be of little value. Instead, we found super-athletes *always* used combinations of performance goals and result goals.

What does all of this mean? It means that super-athletes rarely, if ever, have goals such as "I want to do the best I can." Neither do they simply "want to win." For them, these are incomplete goals that serve no function. The super-athlete prefers to add a result to the performance goal: "I want to do my best so I can break the record." If either component is lacking, success is unlikely. So beware! Without a result in mind, you can lose direction and commitment. If you are looking too far ahead to a result, you run the risk of losing focus. It is a delicate balancing act, isn't it?

COMPARING THE GOALS OF SUPER-ATHLETES WITH OTHERS'

How do the goals of super-athletes differ from those of ordinary people? Take any simple competitive situation. How would you approach it? What would be your goals?

Here are some possibilities:

- Play and have fun (approach goal)
- Prove my worth to myself (avoidance or approach goal)
- Relax and enjoy the game (approach goal)
- Have others accept me (avoidance goal)
- Exhibit good sportsmanship and respect my opponent (approach goal)
- Don't lose (avoidance goal)

Notice first of all that the goals include both approach goals and avoidance goals. What we find particularly interesting about these goals is that, taken by themselves, they appear to be of little importance to super-athletes. One thing the goals have in common is a distinct lack of intensity. Where is the focus? Where is the aggressiveness? They are passive rather than active goals.

Super-athletes invariably favor *active goals* over *passive goals*. There is a definite action orientation that shows up in the performance goals that super-athletes set—the efforts required for them to achieve their goals, both big and little. This action orientation is directed toward the results that the athletes are trying to achieve. Instead of the "frozen" picture of a home run or a touchdown or a long putt rolling into the cup, super-athletes set goals that involve them acting in certain ways—performing the acts that will lead to success.

These goals always include a positive outcome and what they want to happen. So, the hitter might have a goal of making an optimal swing through the strike zone; the runner might have a goal of accelerating into the hole his linemen make; and the golfer might focus on the steps involved in making an optimal putting stroke. Again, even though they may have some type of avoidance goal, super-athletes also focus on approach goals as well as the small competition goals that help them meet their avoidance goals.

Although super-athletes often have approach goals that emphasize either performance ("put the bat on the ball") or results ("win more games"), they do not choose pure performance goals (those that have little or no regard for results) or pure result goals (those that ignore processes). Although they work hard to avoid failure, they do not embrace goals that simply reflect a desire to avoid failure, such as "don't lose."

The message is clear. To enhance motivation, you should choose active positive approach goals and active negative avoidance goals that really matter to you. Although super-athletes generally seem to prefer approach goals, they do on occasion have negative avoidance goals. However, they are confident in their ability to do what is necessary to avoid the negative outcome of such goals.

APPROACH OR AVOIDANCE

When you compete, what is your attitude like? On the day of a competition, are you eager to get to the playing field and get started? Maybe you just can't wait to get started, to go out there and start hitting serves. Or, do you find yourself wishing you really didn't even have to take part in the competition on this particular day? Your opponent may be very talented and you might be worrying that your winning streak may come to an end. You can be focused on what you want to have happen (*an approach goal, like winning*) or what you don't want to have happen (*an avoidance goal, like losing or being embarrassed*). For a golfer, an example of an approach goal is "put the ball on the green." An example of an avoidance goal is "don't miss this putt." Desire or fear—those are the choices. Both can be useful motivational tools. There are dramatic differences, though, in the ways they affect us.

Take a real life example. Suppose you turn a corner and are confronted by a large, snarling dog. Your heart beats rapidly and your breathing becomes deeper. You may be momentarily disoriented, but what happens when you think about trying to avoid something that scares you, but also lies in the future? Suppose you are walking home and you know that you have to go by the house where that same dog lives and that it may run out and confront you. The negative situation hasn't arrived yet, so your fear is attached to a goal: you want to avoid that which frightens you. This is an avoidance goal. You want to avoid something negative that might happen to you. In this case, fear is experienced more as a thought or image about what might happen rather than just an immediate feeling.

Take the example of making a speech or presentation. This is one of the most common fears in America. There is an audience. Your goal may well be to avoid failure or embarrassment. Failure and embarrassment are meanings—more than just a simple reaction to something that startles you, like the dog in the above example. Because the object of your fear (failure or embarrassment) lies in the future, much imagination can come into play here. You may imagine the audience laughing at a mistake you make or being disinterested in your presentation and talking among themselves while you are making your speech. Both of these scenarios can lead to strong emotion. Uncertainty, fear, and anxiety can flood your experience and performance.

Suppose you fear something and want to avoid it. Even with this avoidance goal, if you are confident you will be able to avoid that which scares you, you can still feel secure. If you know you can drive home, the dog can't harm you. If you can walk another route to your house, the dog won't be a problem. However, if you feel uncertain of your ability to avoid what frightens you, then potentially crippling emotions such as anxiety and depression can occur. If you are uncertain that you can keep from making mistakes (the audience will laugh) or if you are uncertain you can make the presentation interesting (the audience will ignore you and talk among themselves), you will more than likely experience anxiety.

Simply put, this means we have two basic kinds of goals: *those that are based on fear* (avoidance goals) and *those that are based on desire* (approach goals). Let's now look at an example from the world of sports to make this a bit clearer. We can't tell you how many times we have heard baseball relief pitchers complain about the instructions they receive from coaches and managers during trips to the mound. Too often, the pitchers said, their instructions focused on what not to do. "Don't give him a good pitch; don't hang a curve ball; don't walk him." Invariably, the pitcher would be left scratching his head after such a visit, thinking, "Why did he ever mention that? Now it's on my mind. Because I'm trying to make it not happen, it probably will happen."

For these relief pitchers, avoidance goals were created. It's like someone ordering you not to think of a pink elephant. The moment you hear the suggestion, what happens? You can't help but envision a pink elephant. For the pitchers, the tendency was for the ball to go precisely to the place where they did not want it to go. The human mind works in such a way that we cannot not think of something. We once jokingly mentioned to San Francisco Giants catcher **Bob Brenly** that when a hitter fell behind in the count, Brenly should say to him, "Gee, I hope you don't blow it and strike out"—just to plant the seed. The mere thought of failure can steer performance. Indeed, the desire to avoid failure, if not used properly, can act as a powerful magnet for failure.

FEAR IN SUPER-ATHLETES

Most super-athletes are fueled by approach goals—big, challenging goals that refer to mastery, achievement, and competence. In addition, they have Little Goals—competition goals that are small and concrete, like "making a good swing," "taking what the defense gives me," or "winning." Most often, as seen in the above list, competition goals are of the approach type, and they are supported by their Big Goals that provide the intensity needed to fulfill them.

Often, though, there is some component of an avoidance goal found in the super-athlete. In other words, *desire and fear join forces to motivate*. The desire for the goal is increased. Intensity increases, and fear can become an ally that is used to make the super-athlete "hungrier" and more aggressive. **Cus D'Amato**, the late trainer of **Floyd Patterson**, **Jose Torres**, and **Mike Tyson**, talked about how fear, if controlled, could work to a fighter's advantage. If not controlled, it could consume him. He was talking about the way fear can energize a person and make that person more alert. However, that increased energy and alertness must be effectively channeled into action. If the fighter focused on his fear—worrying about what might happen, he was in trouble. On the other hand, if the fighter focused on what he should be doing, the fear provided the energy and motivation to be successful. We have found this to be true of the super-athletes we interviewed. They often reported worries and anxieties. However, at the moment of truth, during the heat of battle, they were focusing on their competition goals, what they had to do to be successful and avoid that which they feared.

In addition, through not resisting their fear, sometimes even absorbing it and making it a part of themselves, super-athletes enhanced their performance.

Look at the type of avoidance goals that super-athletes include in their motivations. Michael Jordan and Wayne Gretzky both mentioned defending their reputations. Jim Brown, Charles Barkley, and Joe Namath all mentioned a powerful fear of failure. Larry Bird felt like he had to continuously go "full throttle" to stay on top and keep from slipping back. Chris Evert said she was obsessed with winning at tennis, "... because I hate to lose, not because of the thrill of victory." For judo champion Doug Rogers, "... losing was like dying."

You can see that super-athletes are not necessarily fearless; however, there is something unique about their fear-driven goals. *They do not doubt their ability to avoid that which they fear.* Instead, they are obsessed with avoiding the possibility that they might not give a complete effort and thus disappoint themselves, their fans, and their teammates. Many super-athletes report feeling as if others depend on them. While some of their goals might include fear and avoidance, super-athletes rarely feel they can't do what is necessary, and that is the key. At the moment of action they are focused on doing what they believe they can do—and not on what might happen if they fail. They might have thoughts about "letting their teammates down." However, at the moment of competition they are really just thinking about what has to be done and what their immediate Little Goal is, and this Little Goal is something they are very confident they can achieve. They are not confused. They know what to do. Their concern is much more centered around not letting themselves slip than it is on letting someone else down. They are focused on their own efforts in order to avoid something they do not want to happen.

SUMMARY

Much of the success of super-athletes is related to their motivation. They have a competitive fire that drives them harder than most other athletes. This competitive drive is shown in their *Big Goals.* Super-athletes usually respond to challenges in a positive manner. In fact, many super-athletes relish a challenge—the bigger the better. It is the challenges that bring "spice" into their competitive lives. Meeting challenges is what allows super-athletes to meet their most basic and essential goals.

We discovered that super-athletes responded to three different forms of challenges: *mastery, achievement,* and *competence.* Mastery is the process of acquiring and perfecting a skill. Achievement is the accomplishing of ever greater results, as indicated on the scoreboard on any particular game. Competence is being able to do a task—the perfected skill that you can now depend on, game after game. Super-athletes are motivated by meeting these types of challenges.

Super-athletes also use what we term *Little Goals*. These are goals that are under their control, goals that, when met, help super-athletes meet their Big Goals. Instead of focusing on *result goals*, super-athletes focus on moment-to-moment activities that they are confident they can perform well. These are also called *performance goals*, as opposed to winning, scoring, getting a hit, etc.—*achievement goals,* which are not always under an athlete's control. Big Goals are the driving force in super-athletes, and Little Goals are the moment-to-moment steps taken to meet the Big Goals.

We also discussed *approach goals* and *avoidance goals*. The former are motivated by desire and the latter by fear. Many super-athletes are, in fact, partially motivated by fear, but deal with it in effective ways. Most often their chief worry is that they might not give the type of effort they need and thus disappoint themselves, teammates, and fans. At the moment of competition, however, they are focused only on what they need to do to reach their goals. They have the utmost confidence in their ability to do what they need to, including making the type of effort needed to be successful.

TEN POINTS ON WINNING WITH MOTIVATION

1. START NOW

If you want to be a champion, this is the time to start honing your skills. Wade Boggs, Wayne Gretzky, and Tiger Woods all started to fine tune their skills at an early age and just kept on keeping on.

2. FOCUS ON SUCCESS

Allow yourself to fantasize about being the champion you aspire to be. Take some quiet time and relax into your favorite chair or sofa and use your Focus Edge to imagine the details of what it's like to be the champion you know you can be. Let the details grow so that you really feel them as if they were real.

3. DISCOVER YOUR BIG GOAL

Take some private time to think about what your Big Goal is so you can keep this as a constant reminder of why you're dedicating yourself to this demanding discipline of becoming a champion. Is it the need for mastery (like Ted Williams), proving your talent to doubters (like Wayne Gretzky), or the intensity of competition (like Michael Jordan)? Whatever it is, it's important that you acknowledge this and use your Focus Edge as a motivating factor when the going gets tough.

4. GAIN MASTERY OVER YOUR SPORT

Ted Williams studied the mechanics of hitting and the habits of opposing pitchers. Johnny Unitas studied football films for hours on end. What can you learn about your sport that will put your focus over the edge into championship status?

5. USE SUCCESSIVE LEVELS OF ACHIEVEMENT AS MOTIVATORS

As you gain proficiency in your sport, use small steps of success as markers of your path to champion status. Dallas Cowboys running back, Emmitt Smith, collected footballs from every game he played and recorded his accomplishments for that game on each. How can you make concrete reminders of your success as you grow more accomplished in using your Focus Edge?

6. QUICKLY LEARN YOUR STRENGTHS AND BUILD ON THEM

No one can do everything perfectly. Learn what you do best and continue to focus on perfecting those skills so that you become the best in that particular skill as soon as possible. If you're a better fielder than batter, then keep practicing those fielding skills so that you approach perfection in that area. If football's your sport, are you better at defense or offense, and within that what are you best at? **Muhammad Ali** was best at letting his opponent get tired and then attacking him. Look at how he made that work for him in his quest toward excellence.

7. GET THE LITTLE GOALS WORKING FOR YOU

At the opposite end of the spectrum from Big Goals, Little Goals are for the moment—what you can focus on in the heat of the battle. As Babe Ruth said, "... swing through the ball." "Be a predator," said Matt Williams. "Pounce on the prey [ball] and hit it hard." "Never lose eye contact," recommended tennis great, Chris Evert. "Never wonder where the ball is going." What Little Goals might work for you to focus on?

8. DURING THE EVENT ITSELF, FOCUS ON THE MOMENT

Sure, you're there to win and that's your Big Goal, but during the heat of the battle, if you're not in touch with where you're at, then you're not completely in the game. As Steve Kiner put it, "... when I am in the process and in the flow, I feel like I am part of everything. It's like a dance." Time is no longer the factor; it's all about being in the moment with whatever you're doing to the best of your ability. All your Focus Edge is on being alert and on your best effort.

9. MAKE YOUR FEARS WORK FOR YOU

Everyone has fears, even champions. What the champions do with those fears is to use them as motivators to put more Focus Edge on their Little Goals, what to do in the moment to succeed. Whatever you fear the most, use that emotion as fuel to fire up your performance to accomplish what you know you can do best. You've already worked on and finely honed your personal skills. Allow the fears to just make you focus on your assets more clearly, but remember, fear only works when you also have total confidence.

10. MAKE SURE YOUR GOALS ARE ACTIVE, NOT PASSIVE

Instead of having the trophy as your goal, make your best effort to win that trophy as your goal. It's not the touchdown that's the goal that helps you win in the moment, but rather the successful pass or run that gets the touchdown; not the score, but hitting the baseball right; not the goal, but making the right pass in hockey; not the knockout, but making the right punch at the right time. During the event itself, it's your best effort that should be your goal, not the outcome. Discipline your mind to make that difference with your Focus Edge.

SECTION II: CONFIDENCE

BELIEVING IN YOURSELF

As professional sports consultants, we've heard it said by coaches over and over again, "If only we could understand what makes up self-confidence and bottle it." It's no secret that self-confidence is a key ingredient for success in sports. In fact, confidence may be the single most important factor in the successes of super-athletes. Despite our familiarity with it in our everyday lives, it remains a mystery to many of us, perhaps even more elusive and difficult to understand than motivation.

From the outside it simply looks like some people have it and others do not, but looks can be deceiving. Some people, who look as if they have it, don't really have it. It's just a show they often put on to try and convince themselves or others when they actually are plagued by strong doubts.

We worked with a very successful distance runner who seemed to be very relaxed and confident. However, just before his biggest races he would begin to think that he would "let the team down." He began to doubt that he had the strength and mental toughness needed to perform well. As one of the best runners on the team, he felt he had to "set the pace" for the slower runners. So strong were his doubts, he would get very nervous and end up vomiting shortly before the race. So, it is difficult to tell, from the outside, when a person is really confident. However, from the inside it is easy to tell. With real confidence, persons have no doubt. Deep inside, they know.

Any doubt can spoil your performance. Can you tell when you have real confidence? Feels good, doesn't it? When you're filled with confidence, you feel ready to take on the world. How do you think super-athletes feel? Superstars have an abundance of confidence.

Muhammad Ali shouted, "I am the greatest!" At times Larry Bird felt that he was the best player in the league. Ruth would say of himself, "As

Ruth goes, so go the Yankees." **Charlie Trippi**, a great college and pro running back from the past, responded, "I never had to prove anything. I was already proven." Jerry West, the superstar of the Los Angeles Lakers, believed that he had a gift and always felt as if he was better than anyone else that he was playing against. Ray Nitschke knew what he could do and never doubted it. "With each progression I gained confidence," said Michael Jordan. Wayne Gretzky would more humbly tell himself that he was as good as any of the stars.

He never saw himself as a legend but rather a good solid quarterback for the system, but Joe Montana of the San Francisco 49ers always felt that he could walk on the field and make things happen. He added, "I will find a way to get the job done." No matter what the score, he was always confident in his ability to come back. There is always hope irrespective of the odds. Before the famous comeback drive in the closing minutes of the Super Bowl, he returned to the huddle and said, "We've been here before. Let's do what we have to do and go home."

Arnold Palmer said that he knew his game and the course down to the yard. Football great Jim Brown said, "Sundays were mine. I thought—one break, maybe two, I would run wild. By the time I walked on the field, I thought I was *God*. Don't kid yourself, Walter Payton, Gayle Sayers, all the top runners felt that way." Then there were those that "turned it over to God," like Hank Aaron. "God is in control and will work things out as He sees best. I have just got to live my life the best I know how."

WHAT THE SUPER-ATHLETES SAY ABOUT CONFIDENCE

Here is a challenge for you. Super-athletes seem to be "bubbling over" with confidence. Read what some of these super-athletes have to say about it, and see if you can discover what they have in common. (All quotes were taken from interviews by the authors with each athlete.)[1]

TED WILLIAMS (Baseball)

In my early years, I didn't have confidence. I just hoped I could do it. I was ambitious and had determination. I also practiced and was thoughtful about what I was doing. All this was important for me to build confidence. Most important is that you build on the little things. Set small goals that you can do and accomplish them.

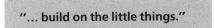

"... build on the little things."

JERRY WEST (Basketball)

I felt I was better than anyone else I played against. This feeling was supported by past successes. I emphasized preparation and my routine. Once I did this I trusted I did what I needed to do. Just focus on the routine and things will work out. I was ready.

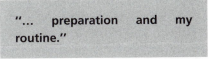

"... preparation and my routine."

JACK NICKLAUS (Golf)

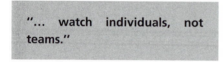

"... know the golf course."

Confidence is believing in your own ability, knowing what you have to do to win. My confidence was developed through preparation. Before a major championship, I might play for 10 days prior to it so that I would know the golf course. I didn't leave anything to chance. When I was prepared, my confidence that I had an edge up on everybody was there. Confidence comes from winning. Starting as a youngster and on up I kept beating guys that were older than me and jumping my own age group pretty fast. That gave me confidence. I believed in what I could do. I kept moving to the next level. Once you go to the pros, that was the last level you could go to. I believed that I could beat them all, so I did.

GORDIE HOWE (Hockey)

"... watch individuals, not teams."

When I was a youngster, I would watch individuals, not teams, in hockey. Then I would try to emulate their moves by practicing and practicing. I always felt like if somebody else did it, so why not I? But I had to produce some to get that confidence. It was the feeling that I have done it, so now I can do it. I believed that if I played at 100% of what I had that day, things were going to work out. I used to mark a stick that I had confidence in. I believed in that stick. I knew that stick was good. And if I was in a slump and not scoring, I figured, what the hell, just get a goal in practice. It proves that I can still do it.

CRAIG BIGGIO (Baseball)

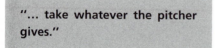

"... take whatever the pitcher gives."

I believe in my ability. My goal is to take whatever the pitcher gives me and adapt and adjust my swing accordingly. I establish a game plan within the limits of my abilities. Realize my limits and perfect within those limits. I would like to put Yogi Berra's statement on my gravestone, "Keep it simple, stupid." You need to realize nobody is perfect every time. Keep it simple and confidence will come.

Y. A. TITTLE (Football)

As a child, I would pretend that I could reach out and touch something at a distance and then I believed I could hit it with a ball. Ever since I was a kid, I could throw a rock, a baseball, a football harder

> "... throw ... harder and farther than anyone else."

and farther than anyone else. I was always good at it. I always did it ever since I was six years old. It grows on you. Growing up in Texas where football is so big, I got a lot of attention. It was a way of life and I had this ability. Football was just part of me. I loved it. Confidence was there because I already knew I could do it.

MARIO ANDRETTI (Auto Racing)

Confidence is feeling sure of myself. I can do the job beyond any question. I built confidence when I was young. Without any experience, I just dove in and proclaimed to myself, "I am a race driver." I was driven by

> "... do the job beyond any question."

my desire. We started building our own cars. There were no Ferraris but I realized I could get in one of these cars and drive it. It was doable and on the road to where I wanted to go. Confidence was there as I took it step by step.

JOHNNY UNITAS (Football)

I had complete confidence in my ability to carry out the game plan. I studied and accumulated knowledge of the game. I accomplished this in practice by practicing over and over again, hard work. Doing well in

> "... practicing over and over again, hard work."

practice makes the game easy and leads to consistency that brings confidence.

JOAN BENOIT (Track)

Confidence is a belief in myself and my ability. I built my confidence through hard training. I believed there was no one out there working

> "... a very supportive and never pushy family."

any harder than me. The secret to my overall success and confidence comes from having a very supportive and never pushy family.

MATT WILLIAMS (Baseball)

> "Focus ... on ... deep confidence."

Confidence comes with success. How much success? Depends on what is enough for you to say, "I can do this." When I feel consistent and success is reinforced, my confidence goes up. But this is surface confidence. Deep down, I am always confident. I know what I can do. Surface confidence can waver. It is shaky. It has to do with whether or not I will have opportunities to express what I can do. In the past, I would fear that a long batting slump would mean going down to the minors. As long as I am playing regular, I know even if I fail 70% of the time, this is still good performance in baseball and I will have what seems like endless opportunities in the future. Focus is on my deep confidence.

GARY PLAYER (Golf)

> "False confidence is based on fantasy."

Confidence is obtained by hard work and discipline. It means working hard correctly and diligently. It takes time to build up. We must remember that there is false confidence as well as real confidence. False confidence is based on fantasy.

CHRIS EVERT (Tennis)

> "I believe the one who works the hardest will do the best."

Confidence is the name of the game with me. When I am hot, confident, I believe no one can beat me. I find I just have to play a lot of tennis to reach my peak. I believe the one who works the hardest will do the best. I was fortunate to win early with my type of game, so the confidence came quickly. I know when I am ready to play a great match. I feel my body will respond to my mind no matter what I tell it to do.

DEION SANDERS (Football and Baseball)

I feel blessed with ability. I take care of myself, my eating, sleeping, resting, exercise and live a proper life. I know my limits. I don't focus on outcomes or results. I focus on what I can do. I am the key to my success.

> **"I focus on what I can do."**

NANCY LOPEZ (Golf)

It was practice that built my confidence. I would prepare so that I would know exactly what would happen. My father was a great teacher. He was always positive and put no pressure on me. He would encourage practice through creating little challenges to make it fun. I felt like I could do anything if I worked hard enough. I was confident in my ability and excited about results.

> **"... practice through creating little challenges to make it fun."**

JEARL MILES (Track)

Everything stems from practice. If I go 110% in practice, then I believe. I just do it. Once I step on the track, I know what I can do. I feel that no matter what happens in the race, I will feel good about it. Whether I win or lose, my family and coach will always be there and I can always learn from losing. Running is part of me and has always been a part of my life.

> **"... I can always learn from losing."**

JIM RYUN (Track)

Confidence takes time to really develop. I could say that I can run under four minutes. But that was simply a statement, that until I did the necessary work, I didn't have any confidence in. One needs a good work ethic.

> **"You have to buy into the dream and the necessary work."**

You have to buy into the dream and the necessary work. We did little things, abbreviated time trials. We would run three quarters of a mile and then, after a short rest, run as hard as we could for a final quarter mile. By adding these times together, you could duplicate what we thought could take place for a mile run. It gave us a realistic idea of what was possible.

During a race, although my focus was on following our plan, the big goal was always in the back of my mind. And, finally, I attribute my overall confidence and success to God-given talent and tremendous people helping along the way.

DON GARLITS (Auto Racing)

"... focus on what I was doing and not what still had to be done."

It all started when I was three years old and my dad was going to build a fireplace on the house. A dump truck dumped a load of bricks. I had a little metal wagon. My dad told me to move this load of bricks over a good distance and place them near the house. My mother came running out of the house and shouted, "Bill, that child can't move those bricks!" And my dad said, "Oh, yes he can!"

I could only move four bricks at a time in my little wagon. I just kept looking at the brick pile I was building and never looked back at the pile to be moved. Eventually the job was finished. I did it! And you should have seen me. I was all puffed up. From this, I found out that I can do things that may seem impossible to others. All I needed to do was focus on what I was doing and not what still had to be done—a valuable lesson. And confidence was born.

Now, let's look closely at what the super-athletes said in the above quotes. What did they have in common? They had confidence in their abilities. They were sure they had the ability to do what needed to be done to achieve success. They also had confidence that they knew how to do what was necessary to be successful. *They had confidence in both their ability and their skills.* So what do you think now? Is confidence as simple as merely believing in oneself? Do you remember the chapter on motivation? Do you remember learning that expectations and beliefs are necessary parts of motivation? Well, guess what! They are also the building blocks of confidence. Have you discovered what confidence is yet?

Give yourself this simple test. Think about investing a large sum of your own money in the stock market. Your goal is to triple your money at the end of six months. Do you feel you have the ability to achieve this goal? Do you feel that you know how to go about achieving this goal? These are two very different things. You might believe that you have one and not the other. You might believe you have both or neither. However it turns out for you, the result affects your confidence. *If you don't think you have both the ability and the skills, your confidence will be lowered.*

WHEN CONFIDENCE IS LACKING ... HOW TO BUILD IT

After the many interviews we conducted, it became clear that the confidence of super-athletes is related to how *sure*, how *certain*, they are that they have the talent and ability to be successful. Their confidence is also related to how sure, how certain they are that they know how to do what is necessary for success. This "sureness" or "certainty" is at the highest level in super-athletes. Richard Petty, a legend in car racing, said, "Even though I had eight or ten people working with me, I was the one who kept the equipment up and made sure they did the stuff on the car that needed to be done. So I had 100% confidence and certainty in the car." Certainty is at lower levels in less successful athletes.

Certainty can be thought of as a scale, with 100% (total) certainty you can achieve your goal on one end and 0% (total) certainty you cannot achieve your goal on the other end. The area in between the two ends represents varying degrees of uncertainty about whether or not you can achieve your goal. Notice that, at the 100% certainty end of the scale, there is no doubt in your mind that you have the ability to be successful. At the 0% end of the scale, you also have no doubt—you are certain you do not have the ability to be successful. Of course, super-athletes (and hopefully you as well) are seldom, if ever, in this situation. The same holds true for knowing how to do what is necessary. At the 100% level you have no doubts that you know how (have the skills) to be successful. At the 0% level you have total certainty that you do not know how (have the skills) to do what is necessary. For most of us, problems arise when we are near the middle of the scale—when we have doubts (uncertainty) about our abilities and our skills—we are unsure if we have the "right stuff" to be successful.

What we are talking about here, when we speak of confidence, are levels of certainty. The diagram below is a simple, but effective, way to look at this idea of levels of certainty.

100%	50%	0%
Completely certain goal can be met	Uncertain goal can be met	Certain goal cannot be met

Now, take some activity at which you would like to be successful. It can be anything. It can be financial security or having a healthy, happy relationship or winning the club championship in tennis. Ask yourself these two simple questions:

1. How sure (certain) are you that you can (have the ability to) successfully carry out the activity?

2. How sure (certain) are you that you know how (have the skills) to successfully carry out the activity?

Place some mark on the scale that reflects how sure (certain) you are in answer to both of the above questions. Do you know (with 100% certainty) that you have the ability to be successful? Or, is there some doubt (less than 100% certainty) about it? Do you know (with 100% certainty) that you know how (have the skill) to be successful? Or, is there some doubt (less than 100% certainty) about that question? Your answer to these two questions shows how confident you are. Try a little experiment. Pick some goals you have in several different areas. Compare the confidence you have with each different goal. Where do you lack confidence? Is it in your ability or is it in your know-how or both?

CONFIDENCE AND THE LACK OF CONFIDENCE

Super-athletes have no doubt in their abilities. They also are certain that they have the skills needed to be successful. Most of us, however, lack this certainty. We have doubts, sometimes small and sometimes large, about whether we have what it takes to be successful. Let's now talk about confidence and the lack of confidence and how they differ from one another depending upon the level of certainty involved.

KNOWING

Confidence with highest level of certainty is knowing. In this case, you feel, deep down inside, without any doubt, that you have the necessary ability or skills to be successful. Wade Boggs, now a member of the elite 3000 hit club, always knew he could play. "My ability is a gift. I always knew what I could do, so I just go out and play and have fun." Similarly, **Julius Erving** (The Doctor) said, "I don't remember ever having any self doubt about my abilities. I just wanted to go out there and get better and better." "I arrived in Japan in November of 1960," judo champ Doug Rogers told us, "and jumped into the daily training routines and culture with both feet. I had to set aside my uninformed concepts of the sport. Naturally, the rigors of the sport meant that from time to time there were injuries and from time to time setbacks, but rather quickly, I started to get the reputation as an up-and-coming fighter." Rogers knew his goal and didn't hesitate to jump in "with both feet." He had no doubt about his ability.

EXPECTING

Confidence with a high level of certainty, but with some element of doubt, is expecting. At this level you may think you have the ability and the skills necessary to be successful, but some doubt exists. It may be a very small doubt (or larger) but it is there. On the positive side, this doubt helped Jim Ryun realize that "although I expected to run under four minutes, I knew the work that was still necessary to actually get it done." On the negative side, this doubt can set up the possibility for negative thoughts and the problems they can cause.

You might not have the certainty of the super-athlete who knows or expects that he will be successful. This lack of confidence can be experienced as either uncertainty about reaching a goal or certainty that the goal cannot be met. Of course with a belief that the goal is impossible, all hope and effort ceases. However, when there is uncertainty, there are at least two ways that this lack of confidence can be expressed. One is *trying* and the *other* is hoping.

When you *try* to do something, what is happening? You are straining. It can be a struggle. It is effortful. You are *trying* to make something happen. There is tension. You could try, for example, to create a belief in yourself by repeating over and over in your head a positive statement such as "I am good! I am good!" The problem here is that these are just words. Deep down, you don't really believe it. When you have to try to believe in yourself, you are admitting that you don't have that belief right now. Real confidence is lacking. It's like trying to hold a positive image of yourself. You have to keep up the effort. Can you see how shaky this is? If the effort drops just a little, so does the belief and doubt creeps in.

Hoping is another way that lack of confidence can be expressed. At this level people realize that they are really not in control of what is going on. All that is left is for the person to wait and see what will happen. You may wish for a particular outcome to happen but then it's up to something else. Imagine you're in a big tournament and, as you look forward to it, you say, "I sure hope things work out" or "I hope I play well." This also sounds a little shaky, doesn't it? Because hope lacks certainty, it can never be a part of real confidence.

One final note: There seems to be an ever-increasing number of religious athletes. They, too, can struggle with confidence, but the exceptional ones believe. However, for them, this belief is often of a different kind. It is more what you would call *faith*. Gary Player said, "I always had tremendous faith that God would use me as one of his servants. I felt like I wanted to represent God. Talent and goals are on a loan basis from God and could end anytime. It is God's plan." It is not so much a belief in oneself as a belief in divine powers and a God-given talent that will "keep the boat afloat." The confidence is a felt knowing and belief that God will see to it that things will work out the way they should, according to His plan. With this kind of confidence you are merely along for the ride and any successes that one might have are dedicated to God. What you are to do is simply prepare yourself, that is, develop confidence in those things within your control and let God take care of the rest. This, too, can be effective when the belief is based on knowing—knowing one's ability and knowing God.

DEVELOPING FOCUS EDGE CONFIDENCE

Have you ever wondered where super-athletes get their confidence? Are they born with it? Do they do something to develop it? Does it occur naturally? Let's take a look and see how these extraordinary levels of confidence develop.

PERFORMANCE HISTORY

What was your guess? Did you feel confident in your answer? Jeff Bagwell, Hal McCrea, and Matt Williams all agree that confidence comes from having a history of past success that you can draw on. Jeff said,

"Baseball is a game of failure. You will fail often. A successful hitter can expect to fail seven out of ten at-bats. But those few successes are always in the back of my mind during times of adversity. Because of that, I have a belief that I will 'bounce back'."

Michael Jordan said, "When I need to dig deep inside myself, I can do that because I've done it before and it's part of my preparation. I know where it's at, how to get there, what it feels like to go deep inside for that extra push or pull I might need." He added, "I wasn't afraid to take that big shot in the professional ranks—I had made one before in 1982 to beat Georgetown in the NCAA title game. Once I made that shot I was fearless after that. What could be more pressure than hitting that game-winning shot as a freshman?"[1]

Notice what Michael is pointing out here. Sometimes all it takes is a "one-time" experience to draw on. Stop and think for a moment. How many successful experiences would it take for you to begin to believe in yourself? Everyone has his or her own idea about this. You can choose from your past however you wish in order to build confidence. For Michael, it was only this one successful moment that was necessary for him to feel "I can do it." Have you noticed how some people need many successes to feel confident? For others, a single unexpected failure among many successes can be devastating. Really, it is simply a matter of choice. You decide how you remember your past performances and create your performance history.

Hal Newhouser, of the Detroit Tigers, had a great curveball and fastball working one day and struck Ted Williams out on three straight pitches. As Ted came back to the bench, he heard his teammates raving in awe about Newhouser's stuff. Then he turned to them and said, "I'll bet anyone here that I will hit one out the next time up." Next time up, he made good on his promise and hit it out at the deepest part of Briggs Stadium. His recent failure in striking out did not bother him. His performance history was much longer than that one at-bat.

Take another instance with Willie Mays. There he was standing at the plate for his fifth at-bat. He said, "Even though I had struck out four times, I couldn't wait to get up with the bases loaded because they intentionally walked someone to get to me. I felt furious and embarrassed and I told myself that I would make them pay." In this case, Willie was not undermined by his past failures and couldn't wait to show them what he already knew he could do. He had a much broader view of his past performance than those previous four at-bats.

You now see that the breadth of one's personal history is important. For example, many hitting slumps in baseball become extended because a player only remembers his recent string of failures. There was an instance when we were working with a player who was in just such a slump. He had a series of line drives caught among pop-ups, groundouts, and strike-outs. Suddenly he was 0 for 20 and began to panic. He forgot all about his previously successful hitting and even the "good wood" he got on those line drives that were caught. Instead, he only focused on the current slump and frantically tried to alter his stance and swing.

Such reactions resulted in a snowball effect and actually worsened the situation. In another instance, a pitcher forgot his elite status as a major league baseball player and became preoccupied with walking in the winning run two consecutive nights as a late-inning reliever. For the most part, super-athletes appear immune to this rather myopic view of performance. They have a more solid and stable sense of "I can do it."

The lesson here is that *you can choose your performance history*. As Matt Williams put it, "How much success is necessary all depends on what is enough for you to say—I know I can do this." Matt continued, "When I feel consistent and success is reinforced, my confidence goes up, but this is just surface confidence. It can still waver and is shaky because it depends on having opportunities to express what I can do. Deep down I am always confident. I know what I can do!"[2] So it's not merely numbers. You can decide to look at past performance in any way that makes you feel good. Remember, how you relate to your past has a lot to do with confidence. You can undermine or shore yourself up. It's up to you.

PREPARATION

Understand that you may need at least one actual successful experience to draw on to provide the evidence or the proof to convince yourself of what you can do. *Although a single success in the past may be enough to catapult your confidence, repeated successes help to build confidence and make it more resistant to failure.* Does this mean you have to start piling up statistical successes and wins? No! It does not!

This may come as a surprise to you but super-athletes often use practice as a way to experience repeated success in order to increase their confidence. It does not have to always come from competition! Experiencing these successes in practice through hard work and mastering the fundamentals of the game is emphasized by Arnold Palmer and Larry Bird. Palmer pointed out that sinking a large number of putts during practice is a sure way to build confidence. Larry Bird felt very confident because of his ability, hard work, and game preparation. He said, "practice, practice, and more practice." Some days he was known to have practiced his shot as many as 2,000 times before a game.

Jimmy Connors concurred. "I practiced hard and I knew that the more I'd practice, the more I'd win." Finally, Jordan and Palmer emphasize the importance of practicing the matching of your skills to particular situations.

As a child, Ted Williams was completely obsessed with swinging. All the time he was growing up, he was practicing his swing. Of course during this time it might be inaccurate to use the term "practice." From his viewpoint, he simply loved to visualize, get the feel of, and continue to perfect his swing. He loved to swing; he loved to hit the ball. Ted would later become very upset when he was referred to as a natural hitter. This is because he felt that people ignored all the preparation, practice, and dedication that brought him to the point of success. Think about this for a moment. The man who many think was the greatest hitter of all time developed at least some of his confidence from practicing his swing by himself!

Once you have had at least one actual successful experience, then you can build confidence through further *practice and preparation*. More and more you know that you *can do*! Remember, you know! This is not merely a belief or expecting. It is the difference between feeling "I know I can do it" and "I think I can do it." You have concrete evidence rather than depending on trying or hoping. Now this confidence can continue to build. This means that as it becomes stronger, it becomes more difficult to lose it. To build this confidence, Michael Jordan had focused on achieving at smaller levels and taken things step by step. Setting easily accomplishable short-term goals to fulfill your long-term goal would be an example. Do you see what these athletes are suggesting here? Use practice and preparation time to build confidence.

CONTROLLABLE GOALS

What are you confident about? Is it about how to do something or is it something else? How do you choose your goals? Arnold Palmer reported that, "despite my reputation as a go-for-broke player, I have never tried a shot in a tournament that I wasn't sure I could make." In other words, he needed to feel confident first. Hank Aaron's goal, when chasing Babe Ruth's record, was "to give it my best shot."

Notice this goal. How confident do you feel about being able to achieve your goal? We would guess that you would feel very confident. You know that it is within your control to give it your "best shot," and the Babe himself just loved to hit and swing big. Another goal that is within your control: Johnny Unitas, the legendary quarterback for the Baltimore Colts, told us "My goal was to score as much as possible and to take as much as I can get." This goal is very doable because there is no ceiling, no specified result. You can go for it, getting as much as you can. You have control here. "There is a time to stand," judoka Doug Rogers told us, "and sometimes to yield and to win is to take the chance."

Before a game, Jordan would picture in his mind how he wanted to play. His goal was "to envision a big game for myself but I could not guarantee it was going to happen." His Focus Edge and goal were to envision, and this he could do. He was involved with the process, the envisioning, and not only the results, of his performance.

Understand the subtle but great difference between wanting to visualize a victory and simply wanting it. In the first case, you have control because you can visualize a victory. However, in the second, you have no control. There is always an element of uncertainty in winning and losing. Many other factors, other than your ability and skills, come into play in deciding a victory. Factors like the direction of the wind at the ballpark, a referee's call, the performance of your opposition, etc., are not under your control. Luck can play an important role.

However, many super-athletes do expect to win. Charlie Trippi said, "Every time I would take the field, I would expect to win. And if I didn't, I would feel real bad. But my confidence was never shaken. I knew my ability. Winning just wasn't going to happen every time." Because these athletes are confident, they do expect to win, but their confidence does not hinge on the outcome of these contests. Rather, it is based on what they already know about themselves. Their deep goals are soundly embedded within their own abilities and skills.

Both Mays and Aaron agree that it was better for their game to have a *performance goal* such as a desire to drive the ball rather than to hit a home run. Matt Williams wanted to hit the ball hard, and for Barry Larkin, it was to hit the ball squarely. As baseball players, they all felt more control over being able to drive the ball, hit it hard, or hit it squarely. Even with these goals there is an element of uncertainty.

Think about it! You cannot predict with certainty the type of pitch that will be thrown. So how can you control how you will meet the ball? Now the goals for Alan Trammel and Jeff Bagwell have a little more built-in control: for Alan it was, "My goal is to try and hit the ball hard," and for Bagwell it was, "Try to get four hits but don't expect it." Notice, in both cases this is something they knew they could do. They could try! Finally, an even more optimal and controllable goal might be one that Ted Williams selected, that is, to make your optimal swing through the strike zone. This you can learn to do with complete confidence.

Many of the super-athletes chose *effort goals*. These goals are highly controllable. You know that you can make efforts! Bird wanted to go all out and play every minute of every single game. Muhammad Ali felt he was blessed with ability and knew he could win. As a fighter, he was simply to go out and express God's potential through his efforts. "The only way to fail," according to tennis star Jimmy Connors, "is by not trying and sitting on the sidelines because you fear failure." The goal for Connors was to be a completely involved participant in the game and focus on making the necessary efforts.

Jack Nicklaus said, "Golf really excites me only when the course is difficult and challenging. I love competing. The pressure of competition against fine holes and fine players makes me feel very much alive. Life is intensified and the efforts you make under those circumstances come to have a significance of their own." Nicklaus' goal is "to do something as well as I possibly can and purely for the enjoyment of that effort and the personal satisfaction I enjoy when I am successful."[3]

Similar to Nicklaus, Gary Player said golf brought interest and enthusiasm to his life. It was the personal efforts, competition, and the challenges that were important.

Aside from efforts, another type of goal, which is more controllable, is an *intrinsic goal.* Unlike *extrinsic goals*, which refer to doing things for the approval of others, intrinsic goals are those things you want to do for yourself. Jim Brown of the Cleveland Browns said, "I set my standards so high, no one could be harsher on me than I was." He went on:

Sundays were mine and I didn't need any fan, writer, or awards person to talk to me. I knew when I did and I didn't perform well. I was brutally honest with myself about my performance. That is why I would avoid reading the sports section while I was playing. Only I could have a true sense of my performance. To play in the manner I demanded of myself, I needed to forget about stats and cosmetics and free my mind of clutter. I didn't give a damn about trophies and things like that. When I won a plaque, I would usually give it away. Trophies are given by man and I didn't need any man to justify what I did.[4]

Think about it! When you are doing something for yourself, you can be aware of what you want as well as what it takes to get it. That is the Focus Edge—you have access to both the process (trying, going for it, etc.) as well as the desired result. So *when you set your own goals, they are more likely to include both process and result.* For example, "I want to give it my best effort to win." This you know you can do. You can give your best effort and you are confident. Do you see how different this is from goals such as trying to please others?

Now what happens when your goals are not intrinsic and you want to do things to please others? Instead of playing the game from within yourself, you are imagining from outside yourself. When Wade Boggs was in the batter's box, he was oblivious to being the center of attention. He emphasized, "I never imagine myself to be the focal point of others." When you see yourself as others do, guess what? You lose touch with your body and see for the most part your results rather than the processes that lead to it. Emphasis is on results and outcomes rather than processes. You want to impress. Your efforts can be hidden from you, so you just want to win! What kind of control do you have over winning? Very little! Remember, you have less control "getting a result" than "going for a result."

Do you see what super-athletes select for their goals? It is not personal statistical results or uncontrollable outcomes. It is a controllable goal that they can feel confident about achieving.

Super-athletes appear to lump both their actions as well as what they are aiming for into their goals: that is, both processes and results. Think about the Focus Edge like this. Their goal is a performance goal that includes the result. For example, although winning is most important to them, their attention is on the processes (e.g., efforts) that it takes to win. It is as if they are attending to the moment-to-moment task process while being guided and energized by the desired result. They seem to select goals that are controllable and include their efforts and skills. Emphasis is on abilities and skills in order to achieve results. Do you see what is happening here? Your abilities and skills are a part of you. It is simply a matter of unleashing what is already there. This you can do. These are goals that are very achievable.

Let's take an example. For Michael Jordan, "It is just a game—a game I want to win." He went on, "I love to compete and it isn't the money. I like the challenge. If I am going to play, then I am going to play to win. That is enjoyable to me. That's fun!" Notice Michael's goal was to play to win and not just to win. There is something very subtle and important here. He was confident in that he knew how to play to win without putting the pressure on himself that he must win or else. His emphasis was on the process, on expressing his performing skills and abilities. The Focus Edge refers to something he knew he could do rather than a result that he had no control over.

What do you think happens to your performance if you are preoccupied with the result—the winning? Where is your attention? In the case of performance anxiety, it is on your own self-activity, your own performing. You feel tense, "looked at," or judged. Quite differently, the super-athlete is focused outwardly and is involved in the moment-to-moment process while being guided by the intent to win. Attention is on the task process and what it takes to win. Overall, *super-athletes feel in control of their goals.*

PUTTING CONFIDENCE TO WORK

From the confidence that has been built up by their *performance history,* their *preparation,* and their setting of *controllable goals,* super-athletes develop certain ways of being. We have discovered that their unshakable confidence is reflected in a *stable self-image* (picture of their abilities and skills) that can allow them to adopt a more *aggressive attitude* toward their sport, select more <u>*challenging goals,*</u> adopt a more *outer-directed focus,* and establish <u>*positive ways of dealing with failure.*</u> Let's look at how confidence helps the super-athlete with Focus Edge and how it might help you as well.

STABLE SELF-IMAGE

"You can go far if you know who you are." This old rhyme describes a simple fact we found in our interviews with super-athletes. When it comes to their sports, super-athletes know what they can and can't do. For Deion Sanders, all-pro defensive back of the Dallas Cowboys, self-knowledge was his most important asset. These athletes knew their strengths and they knew their weaknesses. The "portrait" they "paint" of themselves is accurate, based on past performances, not on some fantasy or hope.

More importantly, this self-portrait is stable. It does not change from moment-to-moment. Because the self-image is stable, it is more resistant to change. When the super-athlete struggles or fails, doubt does not often appear. The super-athlete sees failure as something that everyone does at some time—not as evidence of a lack of ability or lack of skill. Success/failure and ability/skill are separate.

Suppose you never had to worry about proving yourself. Can you imagine what that would be like? When you have a clear picture of what you can and can't do, you are suddenly free. You no longer have to prove yourself. Now you can be more aggressive, set goals that are more challenging, focus on things outside of yourself, and more easily let go of failure.

Can you see how the story is different with most other less successful athletes and people in general? Their self-image is not as stable. For whatever reasons, they still feel they have to prove who they are, that they are "OK." They are not as certain of what they can and can't do. Moment-to-moment successes and failures can cause shifts in their level of certainty. Struggles or failures often lead the person to have increased doubts about their abilities and skills. They are more prone to wonder how others are seeing them. The more doubt there is, the more the person struggles and fails. The more they struggle or fail, the more doubt they have. On and on the cycle goes. This can all result in a lack of certainty about one's ability and skills. The lack of certainty leads to a lack of confidence, which can lead to lower performance levels.

AGGRESSIVENESS

When you are confident and no longer have to prove yourself, you are free to take on a more *aggressive attitude*. You can afford to throw caution to the wind. Now you can take chances because you're no longer concerned that your self-image is at stake. You're less worried about others judging you and thinking of you in a negative light.

Once after striking out, Babe Ruth was yelled at by a fan: "You big bum, what're you standing up there for?" Babe got so mad he drove the ball over the roof of the right field stands in his next at-bat. Remember, aggressiveness is not simply a physical act. It is really an attitude. In fact, Joe Montana mentioned the importance of getting that initial adrenaline rush over with in order to improve performance. On the other hand, Joe's attitude was to attack conflict head on. Such an attitude was also expressed by Arnold Palmer. Palmer had a go-for-broke strategy. He felt more comfortable attacking the golf course rather than playing it cautiously. Aggressiveness is an attitude and cannot always be detected in behavior.

Ted Williams always lived by **Roger Hornsby**'s advice, "Get a good ball to hit." Hornsby put it a certain way. "They weren't doing it to him by giving him a pitch he could swing at; he was doing it to them by refusing to swing at a bad pitch." Can you see how this second attitude is more aggressive? Similarly, Hank Aaron had the attitude of attacking the baseball. He said, "Don't let the ball attack you! Attack it! You have to be out in front of it." Often great free-throw shooters demonstrate this aggressive attitude by thinking "I am going to make them pay for fouling me!" Many super-athletes underscore the importance of maintaining such an attitude even during practice. Michael Jordan made it a point to play with intensity and aggressiveness in practice as well as in a game. Jordan said "I can't take it easy in practice and then just expect to turn it on during a game." Judo champ Doug Rogers "tried to set a pace that my opponents could not withstand. I tried to be creative so that opponents would not think they had been down this same road before." The Focus Edge worked for him. "If an opponent gave me an edge, I would take it."

What about Larry Bird? "I could be a nice guy but I just don't have time for it. There are games to be won." Larry was a fierce competitor and regarded the opposition as the enemy. Michael Jordan added, "If you are not going to compete, then I will dominate you." Muhammed Ali would work himself into a frenzy before a fight. For these super-athletes, there is no going halfway, no holding back. It is going full throttle with the Focus Edge, and don't get in their way!

The important thing here is that as you become more and more confident, you can develop a more aggressive attitude. This attitude means that you are the doer: you decide. You take responsibility. Remember what we're talking about here. What goes on inside the super-athlete is an attitude that may be hidden and not always obvious in the intensity of their actions.

CHALLENGING GOALS

As we've seen earlier, super-athletes usually choose *challenging goals* for their Focus Edge. When confidence is high, even negative or difficult situations can be perceived as positive. This is in part because when you are confident, these kinds of goals can become challenges. Babe Ruth loved challenges. When he was facing Arky Vaughn, one of the top pitchers in the American League, he said to himself, "I am just cocky enough to believe I can beat Vaughn." For Wayne Gretzky, "The best thing was, people were saying I will never win a Stanley Cup in LA and that I will never win another MVP—just the kind of pressure I love. I've been under it my whole life."

When Chris Evert found herself back up against the wall, where others would lose faith, she would put herself on the line, become determined, and accept the challenge without any fear of failure. She said, "I play better when I am down because I am a more aggressive, more daring loser. If I am down close to a match point, it becomes a challenge."

Obstacles are turned into challenges. When you feel that you "can do," then you can look forward to the challenges and savor the conquests of competition. Do you see how you can turn negatives around? When you know you "can do," then even boos from a crowd can be useful. These boos could even get you excited. You could think to yourself, "They boo because they know I am good and are afraid of me." The more and the louder the boos, the better you feel, but the boos could also mean that the crowd is upset with you and expects you to fail.

However, here again, the confident super-athlete experiences this as a challenge. He thinks to himself, "I will surprise them and show them what I can do." In the first case, he can feel the pressure is on him. He is the spoiler, with nothing to lose. In the second, the crowd presents a challenge because of their low expectations, and because of these low expectations, there is less to lose. Confidence is like that. A difficult situation or a risk is exciting and a challenge for the athlete who knows he "can do."

Imagine you are taking the court against the club's champion tennis player. No one gives you much of a chance of winning. You could view this situation as hopeless or you could view it as a challenge. You could then adopt the can-do attitude and set controllable goals for the match. For example, you might say to yourself, "I want to see how well I do against the best" or "I want to surprise the crowd with a big effort." Do you see how adopting this Focus Edge approach would be easier if you had confidence and were not worried about your self-image or how the crowd might view you?

OUTER-DIRECTED FOCUS

An *outer-directed focus* can become a part of the confident attitude. Because you are no longer an issue, you can now focus on the fans, the game, and being an inspiration for, as well as taking care of, your teammates as did Joe Montana, Larry Bird, Willie Mays, Wayne Gretzky, Hank Aaron, Jim Brown, and Michael Jordan.

For example, Gretzky was proud of his assist record. Jim Brown loved playing "Superman" and setting a standard of durability for his teammates. He added, "I also loved knowing the other team spent a large chunk of their week discussing me; how they might stop me and if they did manage to stop me, they would then tell tales about it. I was the fastest gun in the west." Brown went on, "I never wanted to be seen hanging around the training room, screwing around with doctors. This could all be perceived as weakness. I wanted to be an inspiration to my teammates."[1]

The confident super-athlete thinks in terms of "we." Players like Gretzky could set up plays, kill penalties, everything and anything that would enable raising of the level of his play as well as that of his teammates at key times. Raising the level of play of teammates and having confidence in them can make the super-athlete even more confident about winning. These athletes have an acute awareness of things going on around them and how they are fitting in.

Ted Williams is another example of a super-athlete who used an outer-directed focus. He studied the umpires almost as much as he did the pitchers. He knew the short umpires who would call low strikes and the tall ones who would call the high strikes. Moreover, Ted always sat on the bench before a game to study the opposing pitcher. He felt it was important to study every little movement a pitcher made because, as he said, "We are all creatures of habit, myself included."

So, when you are no longer an issue, then you are no longer worried about proving yourself. You can then put more time into supporting the team as well as studying both your opposition and game conditions. You can create an external focus or outer directedness. This in turn makes you feel mentally prepared and gives confidence an additional boost. Unitas said, "I looked at game films and only watched the defensive team. I studied what they could and couldn't do." While with the San Francisco Giants, Mays studied things like the Candlestick Park winds and pitchers' habits. Jordan would envision the tendencies of opposing players before a game. For example, as Jordan put it, "If Clyde Drexler of the Portland Trailblazers doesn't hit his first shots, he will be dangerous for the rest of the game. However, if he makes them he will not be as dangerous later."

All of this mental preparation can enhance performance through adding further successes to your confidence and feelings of can do. There is an outer focus. No self-focus and proof of self-worth is needed. Think about this. What happens when you're doing something with a lot of confidence? You feel good about your ability. Your Focus Edge goal is simply to express yourself and perform well. Now where is your attention? Is it on your every move or on what is outside yourself? Try it. Check it out! It is most likely to be focused outside yourself.

Now suppose you are doing something with self-doubt and a lack of confidence. What is happening then? Are you preoccupied with getting the result you want? And in that tension, where is your focus, your attention? Is it on yourself or outside yourself? Most likely, it will be on yourself—on your performing, but *when you feel confident, you can afford to forget yourself and focus outwardly on the task.* In this way, confidence becomes an aid to concentration.

DEALING WITH FAILURE

We all fail sometimes. No one is successful all the time. When super-athletes fail they use the failure as *information* and an *opportunity* to better their performance in the future. Remember that the super-athlete's self-image is stable and is not threatened by failure. Because they feel certain of their abilities and skills, they do not hang on to failure but rather *let it go and move on.*

Failure does not create self-doubt. Their self-images are not changed by a hitless game, a bad tournament, or even a bad season. They seem to have the ability to remind themselves of their talents and skills. As a result they seem less prone to long slumps or periods of struggling. Make no mistake. They do struggle. However, they are able to take these struggles and obstacles and turn them into challenges, which only serve to further motivate them.

Listen to what Richard Petty had to say about failure:

> When I lost, I never let myself get too low and when I won, I never let myself get too high—tried to stay on an even keel, run along the middle of the stream. I know how life is with its ups and downs. Don't ever let the bad things get you down so far that you can't work yourself back to the good things. Don't let the good things get so much that when the bad things come, you just forget everything. I always tried to remember my ability and the challenge. That's what it's all all about.[2]

Mark Price added, "When I miss a shot, it is more like disbelief rather than 'What am I doing?' I am not focused on what happened but instead on the challenge, 'What I am going to do?'"

Another good example of dealing successfully with failure comes from the legendary Gordie Howe. He would occasionally be mired in a slump when he wouldn't be scoring many goals. Did he begin to question his ability? Did he start to wonder what his teammates or the fans thought of him? Listen to what he said. "If I was in a slump and not scoring, I figured what the hell, just get a goal in practice. It proves I can still do it."

How easy it became for Gordie Howe to keep his confidence up! Notice that one of the greatest hockey players of all time had periods when he didn't perform well. However, just scoring a goal in practice was sufficient to restore his confidence in his ability.

HOW TO USE CONFIDENCE

What's the next step? You just read how super-athletes build their confidence with the Focus Edge. They are confident because deep down they know what they can do (ability) and how to do what is needed (skill). This is based on their past, what they already know about themselves. All in all, this knowing and the confidence that goes with it are "in the heart" of the super-athlete. Deep down, as far as ability and skill go, they feel as if "it is a done deal." Now let's look at how they use their confidence. This might help you use your own confidence in a similar way.

Confidence can refer to the present moment or the future. In the present moment, you can be thinking about your abilities and skills. Do you have what it takes to be successful? For super-athletes this part of the present is a "done deal." It is finished and over. They know what the answer is. It is a resounding "yes." There is no doubt about it.

As we will see in the section on concentration, this frees the super-athletes to focus completely on the tasks at hand. They can be totally in the present. There is no need to waste valuable mental energy on worrying about talent or skills. There is no need to worry about what other people's reactions will be if they fail. So, for the super-athletes, the present is a "done deal."

But what of the future? What about the results of the competition? Here the super-athlete adopts a different approach. The future is given to no individual. We can never know for sure what is going to happen next. That's just reality. There are too many uncontrollable factors that can affect the outcome of an athletic contest. So, as to the future, there is doubt. There is uncertainty that super-athletes must deal with. How do they do this?

We have learned that super-athletes have a keen sense of the uncontrollability of the future. Therefore, they allow for some doubt in their outlook about the future. Instead of the knowing they associate with their talent and skills, they expect positive outcomes. Mark Price had the top free-throw shooting percentage in NBA history. He said, "I know what I can do and I expect to do it." Without exception, super-athletes think they are going to be successful. Gordie Howe also put it nicely when he said, "... I believed that if I played at one hundred percent of what I had that day, things were going to work out." They make this expectation a part of their Focus Edge goal setting.

Notice that they do not know for sure that they will be successful. Rather, they expect to be successful. This is a very subtle but important difference. Instead of the future being a "done deal," it is more in the realm of "it will be done." Much of this positive expectation can come from having been successful in the past. Super-athletes expect to be successful if they focus on present tasks and meeting small, controllable performance goals. They are practitioners of probability theory. Their theory goes something like this: I know I have the talent and skill to be successful. If I focus on the necessary moment-to-moment tasks, there is a high probability that I (we) will be successful. All-time great Jerry West put it this way: "Just focus on the routine and things will work out."

Expecting (as opposed to knowing) that you can achieve a certain result may provide a big boost for performance, especially if this expectation is drawn from previous victories. Positive thinking and expectations can be very helpful to performance, but be careful here! In your mind must always be the flexibility that allows for uncertainty and possible disappointment. No one can wrap up the future.

So let's look at confidence as it relates to abilities and results. What is best and what is worst? Best is to *know your abilities* and *expect positive results*. In other words, through your abilities, put yourself in the best possible position for good things to happen. Worst is to *believe in your abilities* and *know the results*. In this situation, there is some doubt in your abilities and a mistaken notion that you can read the future. In all, what we have shown here is how confidence can be good or bad for athletic performance. What we want is ability and skills to be "a done deal" and results that "will be done."

Have you ever been overconfident? This is a problem that comes up surprisingly often in sports at all levels. The problem arises when you feel that the outcome is a "done deal." It's as if you have this frozen image of the victory in your mind and that is where your thoughts and energy go. The problem with this is that your focus is no longer on what needs to be done to bring about the successful result. It is already on the result! One of the things that needs to be in focus during an athletic contest is your effort. If you are focusing on a victory that you consider inevitable or even already "in the bag," you are not likely to be focusing on the effort needed to produce that victory. So, as often happens, teams and individuals come out "flat" against a team or opponent that "poses no threat." Coming out "flat" means that there is no intensity, no effort. The win is "in the bag" so there is no need to put out the effort. How many times have you seen that happen to an athlete or a team? How many times has it happened to you?

Overconfidence is a coach's worst nightmare. No wonder they love being the underdog and having to fight to gain "respect." Those are things worth fighting for, worth putting out the ultimate effort for. This is one reason the super-athlete is so willing to accept challenging goals. Easy goals require no effort. Lofty goals require total commitment. *The super-athlete knows nothing good is achieved without effort.* It is a lesson well learned for all of us.

Summary

What the super-athletes are saying is this: *It is best to have an unshakable belief in your abilities and skills.* From there, you know that you can get the Focus Edge. This is the strongest confidence. When you have this kind of confidence you can expect positive results. Remember, results are never guaranteed. Nevertheless, expecting positive results is an important part of the Focus Edge mindset.

To build and have confidence, they suggest that you:

1. Control your own *performance history*
2. Emphasize *preparation and practice*
3. Set *controllable goals*

Once this CAN-DO confidence is in place then the super-athletes display certain characteristics. They feel and express a *stable self-image* that allows them to:

1. Develop a more *aggressive attitude*
2. Select more *challenging goals*
3. Use an *outer-directed focus*
4. *Constructively* deal with failure

Now we've "bottled" confidence, when you really know what you can do. An important point is emphasizing the distinction between the Focus Edge mindset and the super-athlete. They are not the same. The Focus Edge mindset is not the super-athlete. Super-athletes are still people and not perfect. They, too, fail. They lose their fair share. At times they also fail to use the Focus Edge mindset, just like the rest of us. At times they can even have moments of self-doubt. However, they do seem able to use the Focus Edge mindset more often than most. Their confidence does seem to remain strong most of the time.

Ten Points on Winning with Confidence

1. MAKE CONFIDENCE YOUR PARTNER

Confidence is an essential ingredient of champions. Getting it is doable—just practice and practice and practice. If you have the commitment and the discipline, then confidence will become your reliable partner in every game. Ted Williams' path to confidence was "that you build on the little things. Set small goals that you can do and accomplish them." Jack Nicklaus got his "through preparation"; Gordie Howe "by practicing and practicing"; Johnny Unitas by "study, study, and more study"; and Joan Benoit "through hard training." Perhaps Chris Evert said it best: "I believe the one who works the hardest will do the best," or as Deion Sanders put it: "I am the key to my success."

2. TAKE COMPLETE RESPONSIBILITY FOR YOUR PRACTICE

Take complete responsibility for getting the practice done, including the preparation and logistics. Even though you may have others to assist you such as coaches and assistant coaches, the ultimate responsibility is yours. Richard Petty said: "Even though I had eight or ten people working with me, I was the one who ... made sure they did the stuff on the car that needed to be done. So I had 100% confidence."

3. KNOW THE DIFFERENCE BETWEEN TRYING AND DOING

Try and pick up a pen. Now don't pick it up, just try. You can invest a lot of effort in trying without getting anything done. Doing is a decision to initiate and complete an act or series of actions. Often, trying is a decision to initiate but not follow through. When it comes to the practice and effort to accomplish the championship skills and acquire the partnership of confidence, then doing is what matters, not trying.

4. WHEN THINGS ARE DOWN, DON'T FORGET YOUR OVER-ALL HISTORY

Champions don't let temporary slumps get them down. They remember their overall record of successful performance and realize that it's the long run that matters, not this week or this month when things aren't going so well. "Baseball is a game of failure," said Jeff Bagwell. "A successful hitter can expect to fail 7 out of 10 at-bats. But those few successes are always in the back of my mind during times of adversity." Look at the big picture during temporary slumps. Think big when it comes to your self-confidence in bad times.

5. CHOOSE THOSE LITTLE GOALS OVER WHICH YOU HAVE CONTROL

We can't control the outcome of our efforts. But we *can* control our efforts directly. Champions often have as their Little Goals either performance goals—hitting the ball hard or squarely rather than scoring a hit—or effort goals—"to do something as well as I possibly can and purely for the enjoyment of that effort" (Jack Nicklaus), which are intrinsic (done for oneself rather than for others). What Little Goals can you choose that satisfy you and that you can have more control over? Such goals have to do with the amount of effort you're willing to put in and are those that feel good to you.

6. PERFECT PRACTICE MAKES FOR PERFECT CONFIDENCE, WHICH ALLOWS FOR A MORE AGGRESSIVE ATTITUDE TO CHALLENGING GOALS

Dedication to practice over time leads to a stable self-confidence. Letting practice slip leads to self-doubt. Both self-confidence supported by practice, and self-doubt without practice, each build on themselves. Practicing with intensity leads to playing with intensity. An aggressive attitude comes with confidence. "I can't take it easy in practice," said Michael Jordan, "and then just expect to turn it on during a game."

7. EARN YOUR SELF-CONFIDENCE, SO CHALLENGES CAN BECOME MOTIVATORS

When you know you can trust your practice and the skills that come with it, then nothing can intimidate you—not the skeptics who say you won't be able to do it nor the boos from the crowd. Once you've earned your level of skill through dedication and discipline, then the skeptics and the boos just motivate you to greater effort to prove them wrong. "The best thing was, people were saying," admitted Wayne Gretzky, "that I will never win another MVP. Just the kind of pressure I love."

8. GET COMFORTABLE WITH YOUR SELF-CONFIDENCE, SO YOU CAN BEGIN TO FOCUS MORE OUTSIDE YOURSELF

Looking outside yourself means focusing on your teammates more, studying outside factors such as opposing pitchers' habits as Ted Williams did, watching films of opposing teams as did Johnny Unitas, and studying how the winds at Candlestick Park affected the flight of hits as did Willie Mays. Such an outward focus can give you the cutting-edge advantage.

9. WHEN YOU'VE GOT THE CONFIDENCE, FAILURE IS JUST AN OPPORTUNITY TO LEARN HOW TO IMPROVE

Champions use failure as a way to learn how to improve their skills. Their positive attitude says, "OK, I messed up. So what can I learn from this so it won't happen again?" When he missed a shot, Mark Price didn't focus on the negative but "instead on the challenge, what am I going to do?" No one is perfect, not even champions. The trick is to keep learning and what better teacher than occasional failures?

10. CONFIDENCE IS GREAT, BUT OVERCONFIDENCE CAN BE YOUR WORST ENEMY

If you or your team are so confident that you're certain of victory, that may rob you of your vigor to get out there and give it your all. There's a fine line between expecting success and taking it for granted. Expect success but never take it for granted. If you do, you and your team may come out "flat," while the underdog, fighting for its life, then has the psychological advantage to win by putting out that extra effort while you are resting on your laurels. Never take your success for granted.

SECTION III: CONCENTRATION

BEING IN THE MOMENT

You may find this difficult to believe, but it is a true story. It happened at the University of California at Davis when the senior author was involved doing research on pain management and how it related to athletics. A practitioner of meditation and concentration was invited to a faculty seminar, as a guest speaker. Reverend Hamid Bey was purported to have extraordinary abilities for controlling pain and was willing to demonstrate them. Here is Dr. Barrell's account:

After an initial period of lecturing, the Reverend suddenly pulled out a small black box. From this box, he pulled out an ice pick and passed it around. This was so everyone could see and feel that it was the "real thing." Then he motioned for me to come up and stand behind him at the head of the table. I was puzzled when he put the ice pick in my right hand. Then I was shocked to hear him instruct me to give him about a minute and then drive it through his neck.

A minute was up at which time I pushed the ice pick up against his neck but was reluctant to penetrate it. He then placed his hand with mine and we drove it through together. Needless to say, the faculty members present were in awe. There was now an ice pick stuck through his neck as he continued to lecture on his topic. His topic was "Pain is nothing but fear and loss of concentration." There was no bleeding.

When he was asked about his secret for such incredible control over pain and bleeding, he said, "I become quiet and gather myself. I have an image of the sun. I am concentrated on that image even as I lecture." For Reverend Hamid Bey, his secret related to an ability to have *unwavering concentration*. If we were able to hold our attention in this way, many things might become possible.

Confidence and motivation are *not* enough! We have seen how confidence is an important part of motivation. First, you have to believe. Then you can move on. But wait a minute. You can have all the confidence and motivation in the world and still perform poorly. Why is that? Let's take an example.

We recently worked with a professional boxer who illustrates this point perfectly. Early in the bout he landed several heavy punches on his opponent and staggered him. This was an extremely important fight for this boxer because if he won, he would be in line for a title shot. The extreme Focus Edge he brought to the ring wavered for a moment, and he started to think about the victory and what the future held for him. He was on the verge of reaching his dreams and reached back to put a little extra into his next punch. The next thing he remembered was lying on the mat, looking up at his opponent. He lost the fight and his chance at a title shot.

Picture yourself as a boxer! Just a loss of focus for a moment. That is all it takes to lose a chance at the title. So, even though confidence and motivation are crucial for performance, concentration is essential as well.

Remember, you can have motivation for *starting* something, *persisting* with it, and finally *finishing* it. Desire can get you started but to persist and finish, you have to *stay focused on your goal*. Concentration has to be maintained. Can you do this easily or is it difficult for you? Are you here reading these words, or are you focusing on something far off that has little to do with what's in front of you? Are you actually here now reading these words, being in touch with their meanings, or spacing out and only seeing the words themselves, the letters, or just black against white? What is happening to you in the midst of a performance? Are you lost in your head, staring off into space, shaking with fear, or being scattered and just plain confused? How can you stay concentrated? Let's first hear from some of the super-athletes. What do they have to say about concentration? What are their secrets for staying focused?

12

WHAT THE SUPER-ATHLETES SAY ABOUT CONCENTRATION

Read what some of these super-athletes have to say about concentration, and see if you can discover what they have in common.[1]

MARIO ANDRETTI (Auto Racing)

When the event is very important to me, it is easy to stay focused. Before a race, I need my space to collect my thoughts and weed out distractions. *I set out to control my mind around a single objective.* I become

> "... become possessed with being excellent."

possessed with being excellent that day. Only one objective and all my thoughts are on it. When I am in "the zone," I am in a trance and time does not exist.

JACK NICKLAUS (Golf)

I have never had a problem with concentrating. My wife has always kidded that I could be watching television and the house could burn down around me, without me knowing it. I've always been able to focus

> "... never *let* things happen ... *make* them happen."

on whatever I'm doing. I've always had to work on what I was doing and what I'm trying to accomplish. I never *let* things happen; I tried to *make* them happen.

GORDIE HOWE (Hockey)

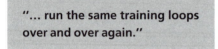

"... see the goal from 'the eyes of the puck.'"

I would always think about what I was doing. Make this most important and block out other things. I could hear sounds of the crowd and my name but no details. Don't let yourself get psyched out by others. One time I did. I heard someone call my mother a name and I went up into the crowd to chase him down.

I like to "open up" and see as much as I can. I have good peripheral vision. And to see even more, I would sometimes see the goal from "the eyes of the puck." This was a perspective that always worked for me on the ice. There was always much knowledge to gather about the game. This is where I kept my thoughts. Two eyes open and your mouth shut is a great way to learn.

JOAN BENOIT (Track)

"... run the same training loops over and over again."

I would run the same training loops over and over again. They became so familiar that I stopped noticing many things. This enabled me to more easily block things out when I was running. *All that was left was to focus on and be aware of my running plan.*

Y. A. TITTLE (Football)

"... never distracted by fear."

I stayed focused by always being involved. I couldn't notice an injury until my goal was reached. I was never distracted by fear. I focused on receivers, and pass rushers did not exist for me. I was a "Bill Clinton"-type quarterback. I was always asking players in the huddle and on the sidelines what they thought, what they wanted to run, and so on. I was into getting as much feedback as I could. *I was always thinking about the game.* It was like a calculation of ideas about what was going on.

MATT WILLIAMS (Baseball)

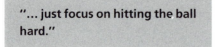

"... just focus on hitting the ball hard."

Have a clear mind. *Only think about the task at hand.* Keep it simple. We tend to overthink. When I am concentrated, things just happen. The speed of the ball appears to slow down. Before stepping up to the plate, I have an idea in my head about how the pitcher will pitch me, what he will try to do. But once I am in the batter's box, I just focus on hitting the ball hard.

JERRY WEST (Basketball)

I didn't even know fans were in the stands. I was focused on the game and us as a team. I would watch the clock and stay aware of the entire game situation. I was very mental. *I could insulate myself and play the game within myself.* My best friend was my mind. I never thought about myself during a game. I stayed focused on what we needed to do to win.

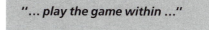

"... play the game within ..."

JEFF BAGWELL (Baseball)

Keeping mind in the game. Taking stock of the situation, how many runners on base and those kinds of things. Focus on what do I need to do in this situation. Focusing on my game plan keeps distractions out.

"... accept failures as OK."

I was in "the zone" for an entire year. There were no peaks or valleys. The key was to accept failures as OK and to let go of them. Ball looked bigger during this time. Focus was on knowing what to do, doing it and could do it tomorrow. There was a belief that I have been there before.

BARRY LARKIN (Baseball)

I only focus on what I want to do and not what I don't want to happen. I don't try to shut the crowd out. I simply focus on my target and the crowd disappears.

"... simply focus ..."

GARY PLAYER (Golf)

Concentration is a result of dedication and hard sweat. I have been in "the zone" on a number of occasions. I remember one time in

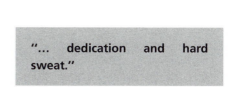

"... dedication and hard sweat."

particular. I reached the 18th hole and I did not know what the score was. *The only thinking going on at that time was thinking about what was at hand.*

Chris Evert (Tennis)

> *"... live only in each moment."*

Concentration is an ability to live only in each moment, not one second in the past or one second in the future. I blocked out all distractions and cleared my mind before a match. Once my mind wanders, the ground strokes shorten, the drop shots drift, the serves float. You can't stand at the baseline and gut out a long rally against a tough opponent when visions of a boyfriend come through your head or you're trying to placate the public or press with gestures, trick shots, and plastic smiles.[2]

Ray Nitschke (Football)

> *"... make something very important to you."*

To stay focused, you make something very important to you. I knew everyone was watching. I had a fear of failure and did not want to fall on my face. This fear kept me concentrated because I knew what I could do. I was confident. I guess if I had doubt about my ability, I would've been anxious and lost concentration.

Ted Williams (Baseball)

> *"... look back and learn from the last pitch."*

I would picture a good ball to hit. I was not guessing. The only pitch you really need to be ready for is a fastball. In the back of my mind, I would look back and learn from the last pitch. I would say things like, "Geez, Ted, you weren't ready for that fastball." *My thoughts were always about what was happening at that moment.*

Stan Musial (Baseball)

> *"... one pitch at a time."*

I analyzed and concentrated on every pitch—one pitch at a time. For me, this was the most important part of hitting.

Nancy Lopez (Golf)

I felt like I was playing alone out there. *I was concentrating only on what I was doing—being in the moment and looking forward to the next thing.* Focus was on something like a putt or a hole. All I knew was that I was out there playing. I knew I couldn't control anything at home or anywhere else but only what I was doing right here on the golf course. I do not remember the crowd.

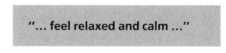

"... being in the moment."

Jim Ryun (Track)

I maintained my concentration through remembering the goal. As I was running there was always that subtle reminder constantly of what I was trying to achieve. Along the way I had a check-off list. At any given moment, I would evaluate, 'Will this help me or keep me from achieving my goal?' This checklist was in place throughout my racing career.

"... remembering the goal."

Julius Erving (Basketball)

I stayed focused by having an embodied knowledge of the game that did not occupy a space in my mind. This knowledge made me feel relaxed and calm and gave me the energy I needed to complete the task. I studied my teammates, my opponents. This helped me keep focus.

"... feel relaxed and calm ..."

Richard Petty (Auto Racing)

Concentration was there. The sport demands it! And I went along with it. If I passed one car and another was in front of me, then my next point of focus was to catch him and pass him. It was a moment-to-moment challenge.

"... a moment-to-moment challenge."

MARK PRICE (Basketball)

"... not focused on what happened ..."

If I miss four shots in a row, I simply tell myself that I just need to
make the next four. *I am not focused
on what happened but rather on what
I am going to do.* Focusing on what
happened would scatter my concen-
tration. In a game I really don't hear a lot. It is like a radio in the background. Just noise, not meaning.

For these super-athletes, concentration includes staying focused on the
game situation, and this means not only being attentive but also having
their minds centered without distractions. Their thoughts are about assess-
ing the current situation as well as implementing a clear plan of action. To
maintain this focus, these athletes seem to emphasize three main things: *be
aware in the moment, make the situation very important to you,* and *organize
your thinking around it.* When all of these factors are present, athletes can
enter what may be called a "concentrated state."

THE CONCENTRATED STATE

Think back for a moment. When have you performed at your very best?
Most likely it was when you were able to keep your attention on the task
at hand, with few, if any, "distracting thoughts" entering your mind. Most
often this happens when persons are engaged in something that is important or very interesting to them (which is another way of saying it is important to them at the moment). Because of the importance or interesting
nature of the activity, your thinking is organized around it. Athletes use
the term "the zone" to describe the concentrated state where activity seems
to be effortless and everything just seems "right." Psychologists have also
used the term "flow" to describe this same concentrated state.

A state of in-the-moment concentration and concentrating, then, are
different. *Concentrating* is an effortful attempt to hold your focus on a certain task, whereas a *concentrated now-state* is effortless attention or focus on
the task at hand and can last for a prolonged period of time. It can be
effortless because the task you are facing is very interesting, important, or
urgent to you and, therefore, holds your attention without much effort or
straining on your part. For example, super-athletes have the ability to make
their goals and what they need to do to reach those goals more important
than anything at the critical moment for action. In nonathletic situations,

you may, for example, find a latest best-seller so interesting that everything else in the room fades into the background. A concentrated state, therefore, is effortless attention to, and full involvement with, what you are doing at the moment. In our work with athletes and our interviews with super-athletes, a concentrated now-state appears to be much more effective than effortful concentrating.

We will never forget the time a player in the National League came to us with a problem. He complained that he would keep losing concentration when in the field. He wanted us to help him. We asked him how he was trying to deal with the problem. He said that he would try to hold focus but then he would just drift off. We told him that if we were able to hold our gaze to the extent that eye movements stopped, we would be temporarily blind. Furthermore, if we become so focused, with that "blank stare," we would tend to get used to what we are looking at and lose attention because of a lack of variety. Seeing involves moving the eyes. So we told him to let his eyes move around the targets that needed attention and not allow them to become fixated.

A few days later he came back and said it didn't work. He tried moving his eyes around and lost attention to what was important. We pointed out there was a problem in our communication and that we did not mean to simply move his eyes around but rather to "look around." He could move his eyes or head to do this. Again, he was trying to do something, concentrate on moving his eyes, rather than simply being in the moment and looking around in a concentrated state of mind. He later applied this information and became successful at maintaining concentration in the field.

The ability to maintain a concentrated state is a critical factor. We recently looked over the many questionnaires that were a part of our interview process for NBA teams during the draft. We were interested in any factors that might predict future success for these athletes in the NBA. What we found was that the single most important factor was an ability to stay present to what was going on and not get "sucked in" by negativity or pressure. Most importantly, these athletes appeared able to control the expression of negative emotions while remaining focused on the task at hand. All of this was further expressed in play that reflected total involvement and abandonment rather than any kind of tentativeness or holding back.

For successful athletes, a concentrated now-state is the preferred mode for *optimal performance.* It is maintaining focus or attention over a period of on-going moments of time. This Focus Edge can be either a *narrowed focus* on one or few things or a *broad awareness* of many things. A concentrated now-state is an ability to feel "at home" and dwell in the moment with whatever is needed.

BROAD AND NARROW ATTENTION

How do you watch TV? How involved are you with what is happening on the screen? Do you notice other things going on around you? Perhaps you are aware of things happening around the house. You might hear children playing in another room or someone preparing a meal in the kitchen. You might see a family member picking something up off the living room floor. You might even notice a neighbor mowing the lawn across the street.

If you are totally involved with what is happening on the screen and not aware of much else, you can be said to have a *narrow field of attention*. If you notice many other things, in addition to what is happening on the TV screen, you have what is called a *broad field of attention*. This means you are picking up an expanded amount of information through just having a larger field of awareness or moving the eyes and looking around.

Do you know what super-athletes focus on when they are competing? Are their fields of attention narrow or broad? Well, it depends upon what sport they are playing, the situation and, in most cases, what position they are playing as well. In football, a broad field of attention can be very helpful for a quarterback. There is a need to see all of the defense at some point as well as keeping track of key offensive players. Johnny Unitas even watched such things as the positioning of the feet of those in the defensive secondary. A broad field of attention allows a quarterback to see the defensive alignment and pickup secondary receivers. However, once the pass is thrown, the attention can narrow.

During a pass rush, Joe Montana said, "I can sense how much red, white, and gold is around me." He knew where everybody was at all times. Joe could always come back to his third or fourth receivers if he needed to. A point guard in basketball needs to keep attention on the play to be run, where teammates are positioned, where defenders are positioned, and where and when teammates need to receive a pass, as well as what the immediate defender is doing. In both of these cases the attention of the athlete has to be broad and include a wide variety of things if he/she is to be successful. Other examples of a broad field of attention could include a baseball catcher who needs to see the scoreboard to keep track of the game situation, the position of his players, and what pitches are working well for his pitcher, as well as any base runners. Elite hitters in baseball often have a broad field of attention before stepping into the batter's box. Willie Mays would check for wind direction and placement of outfielders before hitting.

In contrast, a field goal kicker, in football, carrying out his ritual might briefly look up at the distance of the goal posts and then keep his head looking down at the spot on the ground where the ball will be set down. His gaze might then shift to the ball when it is set down and then return to the ground for a few seconds after the ball is kicked before possibly looking back up to see if the kick was good. His focus is simply on the mechanics of kicking the ball.

Some kickers don't even look up after they kick, preferring to let crowd or teammate reaction tell them if they were successful. Successful kickers most often employ a very *narrow receptive field*. Another example of a narrow receptive field might be found on the pitcher's mound. Here, we can find a pitcher looking down at a catcher's hand for a sign and then the glove for a target. It is like the pitcher and the catcher playing catch with each other. In track, America's great middle distance runner, Jearl Miles, said, "I am not focused on anyone around me. I am just looking at the track up ahead. My worst races are when I see the crowd." Baseball superstar Craig Biggio notes, "Just focus on what is necessary." Two-sport superstar Deion Sanders said, "Focus on what you can do."

We have seen that both broad and narrow fields of Focus Edge attention can be very helpful. The key to success in super-athletes seems to be their ability to be flexible and switch back and forth between broad and narrow fields of attention. For example, basketball players face this dilemma when they have been running the floor and suddenly get fouled and are standing on the free throw line.

Put yourself in their place. Just moments before you were paying attention to all the other players and what was going on around you. Then, all of a sudden, the action stops. There is everyone, moving their arms behind the glass backboard, trying to distract you and make you miss. The crowd, which may have not even been in your awareness, is all at once there in full force. Could all those waving arms make you miss? Not necessarily! You could, as Mark Price, the best free throw shooter in NBA history, told us, use all that motion to help you focus. After all, the one thing that is not moving is the basket. The situation demands focusing down. Interestingly, if the crowd suddenly stopped moving their arms, your attention could be suddenly drawn to them and concentration lost.

Now suppose you are a hitter standing at home plate waiting for a ball to be delivered upwards of 90 miles an hour. Here you need a *narrowed attention* to meet the ball. If your attention wavers just for a moment, you can find yourself simply swinging through air while you hear the ball pop in the catcher's glove. Hitting great Hal McRae talked about shifting fields of attention when he said, "I step in the batter's box, focus down on the ground, then look up at the pitcher to clear my mind. I see the whole pitcher with a soft look. Then, just as the pitcher is about to release the ball, I focus down on the ball with a hard look. I go from a *broad soft* to a *narrow hard* look."[1] The idea is to keep focus in that short interval that ends when bat meets ball.

One thing we found all super-athletes capable of doing was focusing on an appropriate field of attention and shifting back and forth between narrow and broad fields when necessary. During the competition, they most often focused on moment-to-moment or process-type goals and did not pay much attention to result-type goals, like winning. Their attention was only on performing a certain task. At the decisive moment they had a very narrow field, focusing only on the one thing they most needed to do in order to be successful. At other, less crucial times, their attention was broader and contained result-type goals.

ANTICIPATION

Do you ever have the feeling that you know what is going to happen before it happens? It can be a kind of eerie and strange feeling that happens in the concentrated now-state. This is a familiar feeling for many super-athletes. Alan Trammel of the Detroit Tigers said that when he was in "the zone," he could anticipate things happening before they actually happened, and Jerry West of the Lakers felt as if he knew what a player would do even before he did it. Larry Bird, the superstar of the Boston Celtics, always seemed to know where the ball was going to go. He had a great sense of anticipation.

Where does this ability to anticipate come from? Is it inborn? Is it learned? It seems to come from being attentive and aware in the moment.

This means that you are fully present to what you are doing. This means that your mind is focused on what you are doing. Thoughts about what might go wrong, thoughts about what might be happening later, thoughts about what might have happened before, and thoughts about what might happen if you are successful do not enter into your mind in the concentrated now-state. All there is when you are fully present to what you are doing are thoughts about what you are doing at that moment. Because your mind is not distracted when you are in a concentrated, Focus Edge now-state, you can also be aware of all the subtle, little cues that will tip you off as to what is likely to happen next. You are ready. You anticipate instead of react.

When you are aware and in a concentrated state, which way a person is leaning, his posturing, and the direction of his gaze can alert you as to what he is likely to do next. How small are the cues that an athlete in a concentrated now-state can pick up? Defensive linemen in the NFL can look at an opponent's fingers and tell by how "white" his knuckles are whether he will be pass blocking or run blocking. An offensive lineman, leaning with his weight forward to block for a run puts more pressure on his hands and cuts off some of the blood supply to his fingers, creating "white knuckles." The defensive lineman who is in a concentrated now-state can be aware of this because his mind is not filled with thoughts about anything else except what is occurring in the moment.

Johnny Unitas was always looking to predict, to get "the edge." He was so disciplined that he could spend time looking at the feet of defenders, and this type of subtle cue allowed him to anticipate their moves ahead of time. Deion Sanders emphasized, "Play the game within yourself. Stay within yourself and focus on the situation, on what you can do and know what your opponent can do."

When you are in that concentrated Focus Edge now-state, impersonal surroundings can also give you information. An outfielder can pay attention to such things as the strength and direction of the wind. When we worked with the San Francisco Giants, Candlestick Park was notorious for radical wind shifts that would often catch players off guard. Outfielders understood that noticing the wind could enable them to get a jump on the ball once it was hit. It could help them anticipate how far the ball will carry as well as which field it is likely to be hit to. Again, being concentrated in the moment can open you to anticipate the future. Subtle cues are available, and they are all there if you are present to them and not worrying about the past or the future.

Some players are so "at home" with their games that their performances become second nature and they appear not to be concentrating. It's as if they could make a shot with their eyes closed. One super-athlete told us that his hands "see" the basket. These athletes always seem to know where they are on the field and what the situation is. They have become part of their game and are completely involved in the moment—not necessarily concentrating but in a concentrated state of mind. This state of mind includes feeling loose, confident, and relaxed. They are not focusing with awareness, but rather the awareness encompasses them as well as their surroundings. Because of the concentrated state of mind, their *involvement* isn't limited to the present but also extends the present to include an almost magical anticipation of the future, of things to come.

INVOLVEMENT

You have got to get involved. How many times have you heard coaches and players say this? But to *get involved* you have to *be involved*. What does it mean for a person to be involved? It has something to do with your willingness to throw yourself into action with abandonment. Some athletes can do this and others can't. There are those who always hold back a little and keep a distance.

One "benefit" of being in a concentrated Focus Edge now-state is that it allows an athlete to become totally involved in what is going on. When you are involved, you are not standing off focusing on something. It is not like using binoculars. When you are totally involved, there is no separate observer. Neither is it thinking about what you are doing, nor is it playfully enjoying what interests you. Rather it is just doing it. Overall, involvement is an action and means losing yourself in the intensity of the moment. Remember, in a concentrated now-state distracting thoughts do not enter into your thinking. You are focused only on what you are doing and have to do. Because there are no distracting thoughts, you can put yourself 100% into what you are doing. There are no thoughts of failure or injury to hold you back.

The samurai warriors of feudal Japan had a term for this total involvement. They used the phrase *mo chi chu* to describe the attitude of "leaping into action" with no thought of the outcome. Once they had decided what needed to be done, they totally committed themselves to that course of action and gave no thought to the outcome. Even though a failure in their line of work could be very costly, they perfected the art of throwing themselves with 100% intensity into what needed to be done at the moment.

Let's take a less severe example from cross-country running. Suppose you begin the first stretch of your run with a result-type goal in mind—to finish first. As you run, you keep this goal in mind. You keep thinking about it: "I have seven miles to go now."

At this point, you're running in your mind. Midway through the race, you look around and see what a beautiful day it is. You notice the green rolling hills, the wildflowers, and feel exhilarated. Now you're running on your emotions. Then, with a third of the race remaining, your focus changes again. This time you feel like you are "gliding" and running on automatic. You feel your feet hitting the ground and the movement of your chest with each breath. There is an acute sense of your body. You are running in your senses. Now, the final stretch—the last part of the run. There is a hill to climb up ahead. You feel exhausted, but you desperately gather yourself for this last stretch. Up the hill you go. You are straining, charging, and giving it everything you have. At this point *there is no thinking, no emotion, no sensing but only awareness and movement*—the struggle, and this movement completely absorbs you. All there is at this time is the hill, the path, and the "push." There is only the shrinking distance between yourself and the finish line. *You are completely involved.*

TARGETS

The concentrated Focus Edge now-state includes both *involvement* and *anticipation* for super-athletes. However, it also includes more. The *targets* on which super-athletes focus are also present. These targets can be "in the athletes' heads" and refer to certain thoughts they have, or they can be "outside" the athletes in the situations around them. The targets are what they focus their attention on. What targets do the super-athletes focus on? Let's hear from Michael Jordan. "Before a game, I picture the way I want to play. I can envision a big game for myself. But I can't guarantee it is going to happen." The legendary Johnny Unitas of the Baltimore Colts added, "I am focused on reading defenses, looking at details, and making adjustments." Similarly, Jeff Bagwell of the Houston Astros took stock of the situation: "How many runners are on base? What do I need to do in this situation? Focusing on my game plan keeps distractions out."

From focus on thoughts, we turn to a focus on the situation. As Willie Mays put it, "I never think about records. All I do is swing where the ball is pitched. The minute I start thinking about hitting a home run is when I stop hitting one." Once in the batter's box, Matt Williams, the All-Star third baseman for the San Francisco Giants simply focused on hitting the ball hard. For Barry Larkin of the Cincinnati Reds focus was on the process not the end goal. He said, "As a hitter, focus needs to be on the ball and not your body stance. And most importantly, just go moment to moment." Jerry West watched the clock a lot to continuously give him information about the game situation.

Sandy Koufax, the blazing fastball pitcher of the Los Angeles Dodgers, mentioned that he had to be with every pitch. "I knew that every pitch meant something because we weren't going to score a lot of runs." While in center field at windy Candlestick Park in San Francisco, the incomparable "Say Hey" Willie Mays would be focused on the external environment and targets like the hitter and the direction the flag was blowing.

When it comes to targets of attention, super-athletes are focused on certain key areas. Think about it. At any given moment you are paying attention to something. It could be something "inside" you like a thought or a feeling. It could be your physical body. It could be "outside" you in your surroundings. Super-athletes appear able to maintain their attention on whatever targets are necessary to successfully complete the task in front of them.

Many things can throw you off track, if you let them. As consultants for the Orlando Magic, we helped players keep off-the-court distractions from hurting their performances. We all know how issues in our everyday lives can clamor for our attention and threaten to turn us away from our performance goals and objectives. In order to focus and keep your attention on particular targets, you need the ability to *ignore or block out distractions.* How do super-athletes do this? One of these athletes, a client of ours, spoke very clearly to us about his mindset. "I played like nobody was in the stands. That was my thought pattern. I wouldn't think about anything but the ball. I wouldn't look at the crowd whether they were cheering or booing. I learned to focus by meditating. I learned to go to quiet places and just release and let my mind go."

Wayne Gretzky believes one should give the game his all everyday and block out everything else. Michael Jordan said, "I don't focus until game time. I am just joking around, but 15 minutes later you can't say a word to me. Later, I can hear the cheering respect during introductions, but I don't hear anything beyond that." Other common remarks of super-athletes include, "I didn't even know fans were in the stands," or "Even though I knew the fans were in the stands, I did not pay attention to them." Jerry West added, "I never even thought of myself or the crowd during a game, only about us winning." Everything he was concentrated on was on the floor between the lines. All else was ignored. Florida basketball coach Billy Donovan placed on the blackboard a rectangle divided into three parts: to the left was the past; to the right, the future; and in the middle was the court—the NOW (the moment).

In our work as sports consultants and in doing interviews for this book we have spoken to many super-athletes. We have noticed that they seem to approach the process of holding the Focus Edge in the same way and with the same intensity that they approach the game situation. For them, concentration and staying focused is an ability, a process under their control. Keeping focused and controlling what is going on inside them can become a challenge for the super-athlete. They realize they can control what is going on inside as well as influence what is outside them. After all, they are in charge of doing it, so they pretty much "just decide" to take charge of their thoughts. Remember processes, as opposed to results, are under our control, and concentrating and holding focus is just another process.

How can you increase your ability to focus on your thoughts (or on something "outside" of you) successfully? Instead of making an effort to "try" to concentrate, do what the super-athletes do. *Just make the concentrated now-state Focus Edge and its target more important than whatever else you might be preoccupied with.* When what you are concerned about and trying to block out becomes less important, focus will be there. And, if the result becomes more important then the process, desire and fear can ruin what is necessary for your sustained concentration. To sustain concentration can be very special. It most often just happens and you simply notice yourself in an on-going, extended version of a concentrated state. This was earlier referred to as the "zone."

INSIDE THAT ELUSIVE "NOW-ZONE"

The zone seems to be a very special place that athletes readily recognize when using the Focus Edge. When you are performing in the now-zone, everything seems easy. It is as if you are not even doing it. You just intend something and it happens. There is a strong feeling of vitality and sometimes events seem to be happening in slow motion. However, it is the feeling of being right here, aware of this moment, a state of being concentrated, which is extended in time.

How do super-athletes enter the now-zone and remain concentrated? It is one thing to be occasionally in the zone but it is quite another to be able to stay there for a while. Tony Gwynn of the San Diego Padres appeared to be someone who could stay there for long periods of time. His batting averages were well over .300 year after year. Tony was a contact hitter and wanted to consistently keep the ball in play. A natural reflection of being concentrated and in the now-zone is consistency. For Larry Bird, "Consistency is the key. You play your game and worry about nothing else." When we asked Ray Nitschke about the zone, he said, "I was always in it. It was a consistent part of my game." It is the consistency of superior performances that best defines the super-athlete.

Here is what else super-athletes say about "being in the zone." (All quotes were taken from interviews by the authors with each athlete.)

CRAIG BIGGIO (Baseball)

When I am in the zone, I feel prepared and I just go moment to moment—from one doing to

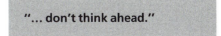

"... don't think ahead."

another. *It is simple.* No thinking is involved. I don't think ahead. All of a sudden, I just find myself on second base and the runners have been driven in.

Mario Andretti (Auto Racing)

| "... like being in a trance." |

In the zone is like being in a trance. Time does not exist. *Things slow down. Only one objective.*

Steve Kiner (Football)

| "... being in the moment." |

Being in the zone is *being in the moment.* No longer on fast forward. Things slow down. In the flow. No longer discrete changes and surprises. Now there is continuity and no surprises. I feel like I am part of everything that is going on.

Joan Benoit (Track)

| "... kind of surreal." |

The zone. I couldn't make it happen. It just happened. It was kind of surreal. I would derive power as I ran hard. Everything was vivid and the *running felt effortless.* I felt very strong.

Ken Griffey, Sr. (Baseball)

| "... hear the ball and see the seams." |

In the zone, *everything is in slow motion.* I can slow the ball down and almost stop it. Doesn't matter who is pitching. It seems like they are always just throwing it right down the middle. I can hear the ball and see the seams. I know what the pitcher is going to throw. I am relaxed and focused on a good smooth swing. I am very quiet "inside."

MATT WILLIAMS (Baseball)

The zone means having a clear mind. *Keeping it simple. Thinking only about the task at hand.* Things are just happening. Speed of ball appears to slow down.

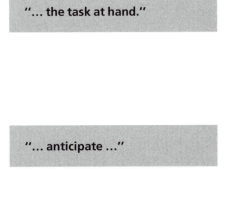

"... the task at hand."

ALAN TRAMMEL (Baseball)

In the zone, *I can anticipate things happening.* I feel "hitterish."

"... anticipate ..."

HAL McRAE (Baseball)

The zone is a space where *I can anticipate.* I know what is going to happen before it happens. I can actually visualize it. It is easy to visualize in "the zone." There are no surprises and no startle when in that space. Being in the zone means *keeping things very simple while noticing and doing one thing at a time.*

"... visualize ..."

BARRY LARKIN (Baseball)

In the zone, there is no fear of failure. It is just a game. In the flow of the game, I feel like I am both doing it and I am not doing it. *Everything is just happening.*

"... no fear of failure."

RAY NITSCHKE (Football)

When I was in the zone, *I got completely involved with whatever I was doing.* It could have been in practice, the game, or whatever. At this time, I never heard the crowd. I felt relaxed and in control, tranquil, and intense. I was ready for anything.

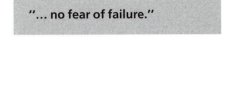

"... tranquil and intense."

Don Garlits (Auto Racing)

"... no sound."

Racing forced me to be in the zone. *Everything slows down.* It is like being in a tunnel. I could see clearly but didn't hear anything. *It is quiet.* There is no sound. But I could see a small muscle twitch on the arm of the guy starting the race.

Mark Price (Basketball)

"... on the outside ..."

I have experienced this flow quite often. It is like "I am on the outside looking in." Like I am not really there. Everything I touch and shoot goes in. It doesn't matter where it is from. *It is like I am not even doing it.* Everything is just like it is happening. Everything is escalated—the joy, the fever of the fans. When I am rolling, everything is magnified.

The zone is a special "space" to be in. Super-athletes describe the zone in quite similar ways. What they say is *keep things simple, consider only the task at hand,* and *be relaxed and quiet "inside."* In the zone, things slow down, time appears to slow down or stop entirely, everything is just happening, and sometimes the future can be accurately anticipated. It's more like letting things happen rather then making them happen.

Sometimes, you can be in the zone for long periods of time. Some super-athletes have reported being in the zone for entire seasons. It is a wonderful "space" to be in, but is most often difficult to enter and sustain. As a special case of concentration, it remains a mystery to most athletes.

HELPFUL RITUALS AND VISUALIZATIONS

What can you do to encourage the Focus Edge and even getting in the aware now-zone? Super-athletes often use *rituals* and *visualization techniques* to stay on track. Sometimes these athletes might come across as hard-nosed, aloof, or simply difficult to deal with. Often this is because they are committed to remaining concentrated on their "package" that is all that they consider important to succeed or win. As part of this package, these athletes may be concentrated on rituals.

A ritual is a step-by-step process that is believed to lead to success. Ted Williams would make sure that he would step into the same place each time in the batter's box. Chris Evert would check her racquet, adjust her dress, and wash her hands before a match. Sometimes these rituals can appear crazy or bizarre. For example, one linebacker in the NFL needs to become nervous and vomit before he feels that he is ready to play. Sometimes a ritual is just a simple plan. Ted St. Martins, a 60-year-old ex-dairy farmer known by his sponsor as the Coors Silver Bullet Sharpshooter, held the Guinness World Record for more than 2,000 free throws in a row without a miss. His ritual included a simple series of steps:

1. Always stand at the exact same place on the free throw line.
2. Hold the ball like you would an egg.
3. Bend the knees only slightly.
4. Take a deep breath.
5. Focus on the back of the rim.
6. Exhale and let the ball go.

Ted suggested just doing these steps and letting it happen: focus on this process and let the results take care of themselves. When we asked Ted about his goal, he said, "My goal is to simply carry out these steps and then watch the beauty of the ball swishing through the net." For him, making baskets was an aesthetic. He could not understand why coaches would reward players for making a series of consecutive shots during practice by letting them quit shooting and go home. To him the reward should be continued shooting. *Focus is easy when you love doing what you are doing.*

The technique of *visualization* may or may not be a part of a ritual. However when it is applied, it can work wonders. Seeing is believing. For Muhammad Ali, to be successful, it is important to know you are good and, if you can't do that, then *pretend* that you are. To pretend real well, have a vivid, clear image; fill in all the details; feel it as well as see it; and practice it over and over until it becomes part of you. Eventually your body will believe what you believe.

It is just like dreaming at night. If you experience stress in your dream, what do you think your body does? Does it say to itself, "Well, this is just a dream and there is no need to fire up the system?" Of course not! The body does fire up and goes along with whatever you are believing in your dreams. There is no distinction between real and unreal.

So, *if you can visualize, then you can pretend.* You can "act as if" something has happened before it actually has happened. Many super-athletes use visualization techniques. For instance, Don Garlits, the famous drag racer, would use it on flights. He reported, "I would visualize an entire process of building a car—all the way up through it's completion. I would just lay the pipe on the jig in my mind and go from there." There are different perspectives available depending on the athlete and the situation. For example, as a baseball hitter, would you rather be visualizing yourself from the viewpoint of the pitcher, from behind the plate, opposite you in the batter's box, behind yourself, or in your body looking out at the pitcher?

These are all options for the Focus Edge. However, all the perspectives are from an outer viewpoint but the last. An outer viewpoint means looking at your body from an outside perspective. Most of the super-athletes suggest including an *outer viewpoint* when learning a skill, an *inner viewpoint* when actually performing and both when trying to correct a flaw in performance.

SUMMARY

What makes up *concentration? Attention and its targets* are certainly part of it. Yet there is also *anticipation and involvement.* Although you are immersed in the momentary situation, there can also be a rather eerie sense of knowing what is going to happen next. Concentration (concentrated now-state) seems to be a subtle mixture of being in the moment, seeing as much as you need to see, and preparation for what is coming. To keep the Focus Edge going, and possibly even entering "the now-zone," you may need to ignore or block out distractions. To do this, being preoccupied with your game plan, which may be supported by a method like *visualization*, can be very helpful. The important thing is focusing and maintaining it.

Effective concentration also requires *flexibility*. You need to be able to go from a *broad to a narrow field of attention*. For the super-athlete, flexible attending takes place within a state of concentration. In this state, there is complete involvement and an ability to anticipate. You are in the moment and ready for the future, and your targets during this state refer to focus on the momentary task. As Jearl Miles put it, "When I am concentrated, I am aware of myself. I have a plan and want to execute it."

Focus on what you can do. Although super-athletes aim for results, *they focus on process*. Process depends on our own efforts and leads to confidence because we feel as if we're able to do what it takes. After all, process belongs to us. Confidence then makes it easier for us to stay on track without wavering with doubt and fear. When process is very important to us, then we are motivated, and when motivation is directed at process, it too helps us stay focused and concentrated. If we sustain concentration, it might even lead us to "the now-zone."

TEN POINTS ON WINNING WITH CONCENTRATION

1. MOST IMPORTANT FOR WINNING IS BEING IN THE MOMENT

Winning, for Jack Nicklaus, meant being "totally aware of where I am and what I am doing and what I am trying to accomplish." For Chris Evert, it meant "an ability to live only in each moment, not one second in the past or one second in the future." Ted Williams said, "My thoughts were always about what was happening at that moment." Championship racing for Richard Petty "was a moment-to-moment challenge." For successful wins over time, being in the moment is essential.

2. WHY "BEING IN THE ZONE" OR "FLOW" ARE SO IMPORTANT

Of course you've heard of "being in the zone." It's when champions lose track of the outside world and are totally immersed in the moment of the game. They become transformed into beings approaching perfection as they call on their deepest resources to accomplish the best they can under challenging circumstances. Psychologists call this phenomenon "flow," an enjoyable flow of creative effort when time seems to stand still. If you want to become a champion, become familiar with these terms and let yourself experience them.

3. LEARN ABOUT BOTH BROAD AND NARROW FIELDS OF ATTENTION AND HOW TO SHIFT BETWEEN THEM WITH FLEXIBILITY

A quarterback needs to know who's out there to receive his pass, where his secondary receivers are, and who's rushing him at that very moment— all this almost at the same time. That's broad field of attention. However, when he finally decides to throw the ball, his focus shifts instantly to a narrow field of attention—exactly how he should deliver that pass, given how the receiver is covered, wind factor, and how quickly he can get that pass off as he's being rushed. That's narrow focus. If he can shift from one to the other very quickly, he's champion material. Practice both fields of attention and the flexibility to go between them.

4. BE IN THE MOMENT, AND YOU CAN ALMOST PREDICT THE FUTURE

There's something about being totally present in a game that allows champions to get a sense of what's about to happen. Wayne Gretzky was famous for skating where the puck was going to be. Sure, there are certain cues that give the future away—white knuckles of linemen sometimes reveal their intentions. Leaning forward, with more pressure on their knuckles may mean they're intending to block for a run rather than a pass. But sometimes the cues aren't that obvious. However, when there is an awareness that the edge of the future is ready to enter, let yourself be in the moment and react to cues that are difficult to put into words.

5. MAKE LIKE A SAMURAI—THROW YOURSELF IN 100%

Even more extreme than just being in the moment, throwing yourself in 100%, as the samurai did, means you're giving your all, no matter what the outcome. Of course, you can't do this all the time, but when champions come to that defining moment, as in the last minutes of a tie game, then it's time to get involved 100%, holding nothing back, as if this were your dying moment. As Doug Rogers put it, "Losing was like dying." It's during moments like this that sports history is made. Learn what it's like to be a samurai—especially when it counts.

6. BEING IN THE MOMENT MEANS CLARITY OF FOCUS

When you're in the moment, your focus is on only one thing, the processes that relate to winning. "All I do is swing where the ball is pitched," said Willie Mays. "The minute I start thinking about hitting a home run is when I stop hitting one." All distractions are blocked out. Once the game started, Michael Jordan had that focus: "I can hear the cheering respect during introductions, but I don't hear anything beyond that." Just focus on what you need to do, not the crowd, not your family, not even your coach—at that significant moment!

7. BEING IN THE "NOW-ZONE" MEANS GOING WITH THE FLOW

Once you're in the "now-zone," things can become quite easy and natural. Your mind and body are one. Your intentions become reality, it seems, without even thinking about it. There's a natural flow between what needs to be done and its happening without your even thinking about it. "It seems unconscious," said Craig Biggio; "like being in a trance," said Mario Andretti. Steve Kiner described it as "continuity and no surprises." "It was kind of surreal," said Joan Benoit. "Everything was vivid and the running felt effortless." "In the zone, there is no fear of failure," said Barry Larkin. "I feel like I am both doing it and I am not doing it. Everything is just happening."

8. THERE IS A PLACE FOR RITUALS

Some super-athletes depend on rituals that help them get a feeling of control in order to reduce the sense of stress that may come with competitive challenges. It's human to feel more comfortable with a sense of control. Rituals fit that bill. Ted Williams' stepping into the same place at the batter's box, Chris Evert's hand-washing ritual helped them both feel more at ease in highly stressful situations. Though these actions fall into the category of superstitions, they may help certain athletes, including champions, to perform better with less stress, especially if they happen to be sensitive to stress. Respect others when they engage in such rituals. You may end up using them yourself.

9. VISUALIZATION IS A PROVEN TECHNIQUE FOR ATHLETIC EXCELLENCE

Some years ago, a psychologist found that Olympic weight lifters could improve their performance merely by imagining going through the repetitions of lifting weights in their minds. Since then, more athletes have benefited by using such visualizations. It turns out that the brain reacts to mental rehearsal as well as to physical practice. Going over the physical motions of your sport movements in your head helps your body become more fluent in those motions. Guy Lafleur, NHL hockey great, would spend some time before a game sitting in the bleachers and going over the game he hoped to play. It worked for him. It can work for you.

10. BEST PRACTICE OF VISUALIZATION INVOLVES BOTH INNER AND OUTER VIEWPOINTS

Looking at your body from the outside is the outer viewpoint. The inner viewpoint means experiencing from your own bodily perspective. Use the outer viewpoint when learning a skill, the inner when actually performing it, and a combination when correcting a flaw in your performance. Visualization allows you to rehearse your moves without leading to fatigue, so a combination of visualization and actual practice puts you ahead of the game.

SECTION IV: PRESSURE SITUATIONS

16

WHERE IT ALL COMES TOGETHER, UNDER PRESSURE

What is it that makes super-athletes super? If there is one skill that sets them apart from the rest, it is their ability to deal with *pressure situations*. When there are only a few seconds left in a championship game, who will make the winning shot? In the bottom of the ninth with two outs, who will get the game-winning hit? Who will sink the long putt on the 18th hole of a major golf championship? In most cases the answer to these questions is … the super-athlete. Almost by definition the super-athlete is one who can consistently produce in pressure-packed situations when everything is on the line.

Of all the facets of the Focus Edge, dealing with pressure is the most fascinating. Every athlete, even the weekenders among us, faces such types of situations. Some athletes seem able to do everything "right" when it's most important, while others never seem able to produce in the "clutch." What is the secret to the super-athletes' success in pressure situations? We have discovered, through numerous interviews, how elite athletes deal with pressure-type situations. They seem to share some very simple, yet effective, techniques that enable them to perform at their best when it counts the most. In addition, we have found that these simple techniques can be used by any of us ordinary athletes or even nonathletes to deal with the pressure situations we experience in our own lives, both on and off the field.

Let's start with a riddle. How can someone be "under pressure" and be having fun at the same time? Think about this. It doesn't seem to make sense. A pressure situation is a time of great uncertainty, where things could go either way, and the stakes are high. There's a lot to be won or lost, and the outcome is in serious question. How can someone enjoy a situation where there's so much to lose and the outcome seems to hang on a thread?

The answer to the above riddle lies in the "inside" game. Listen to what Jack Nicklaus said about pressure. "Pressure doesn't mean anything to me. Pressure situations are what I strive to get involved in. The whole idea is to practice and prepare so that when I am coming down the stretch and supposedly under pressure, it becomes fun. Pressure is the fun of the game." Jack has developed a way of looking at tough situations so that they don't intimidate him. In fact, he looks forward to pressure situations. Giving 100% to meet the challenges of a pressure situation is what he looks forward to. Testing himself in this way is fun for Jack.

The above quote sends us, once again, to the "inside" game for the answers to our questions. However, before we delve into how super-athletes deal with the performance anxiety that affects so many of us, it might be helpful to look at a couple of questions we will be asking in this chapter. First, *what is pressure and what is the difference between pressure and a pressure situation?* The actual pressure situation is very different from the feeling of pressure. Second, *what causes performance anxiety?* Are these causes outside or inside us?

Once we've done this, we will then look at how super-athletes respond to pressure situations. This relates to how they view crunch time or critical situations in competitive sports. In some ways super-athletes remove the cause or causes of performance anxiety. How do they do this? Next, we'll look at the super-athlete solution for reducing performance anxiety. What do these elite performers share as parts of an effective mindset? Finally, how can the super-athlete solution be applied? What can you do with this information to reduce your own performance anxiety?

THE DIFFERENCE: PRESSURE AND PRESSURE SITUATIONS

If we go back and look at the above quote from Jack Nicklaus, it becomes clear that pressure and pressure situations are two very different things. Jack was in many pressure situations, but he did not experience pressure to the degree that many of us do. Pressure is what people also call *performance anxiety.* For many people, the experience of performance anxiety includes sweaty palms, "butterflies" in the stomach, rapid heartbeat, and other physical symptoms. It may also include disruptions in concentration. So, the feeling of "pressure" refers to *our experience of a set of physical responses.*

A pressure situation, on the other hand, is simply *a situation in which there is something important at stake and the outcome of the situation is uncertain.* There may be money at stake. There may be a championship at stake. There may even be self-esteem or self-respect at stake. It is the combination of *uncertainty* and *importance* that leads to the experience of pressure or performance anxiety.

Let's look at some situations in sports that are often thought of as pressure situations. You're up to bat. It's the bottom of the ninth, there are two outs, and the bases are loaded. Your team is trailing 3-2 in the championship game. The pressure is on, right? How about this one? Your basketball team is behind by a single point. You're fouled as time runs out. You'll be shooting one and one free throws. Your team can either win (if you sink both) or lose the title if you miss the first. Can you feel your heart beating faster as the championship is on the line? Here is yet another possibility. Your football team is down by two points and there are only two seconds left in the game. You are about to kick a field goal, a "chip shot" that everyone expects you to make. The opponents call time out, and you are left with almost two minutes to think about the kick. What are you feeling in this situation?

For many athletes, these are moments of extreme stress and performance anxiety (pressure). However, for others, these moments are not only not stressful, but they actually bring out the athletes' best. It is clear that performance anxiety can seriously hamper performance, so it is important to learn how to avoid it. In order to do this, to learn how to avoid performance anxiety, we first need to learn how we create it in ourselves.

HOW WE CREATE PERFORMANCE ANXIETY

What causes performance anxiety? It does not just depend on the situation you are in. If that were the case, Jack Nicklaus and other super-athletes would be in the same boat as the rest of us. They encounter pressure situations whenever they play and yet they experience little performance anxiety. So, performance anxiety is not "out there." It is experienced as being "inside us." What stirs it up inside us? Is it our nerves? Is it our hormones? Our muscles tightening? In part, yes. But what is behind these physical feelings we experience as performance anxiety?

Some years ago, a groundbreaking study was conducted that showed how people create performance anxiety inside themselves. The study required that people *learn how to observe the flow of their thoughts.* These observations were to be made at the time the performance anxiety was actually being felt.

Descriptions of these experiences of performance anxiety were collected, and elements common to all of the experiences were identified. These common elements or necessary conditions represented the causes of the experience of performance anxiety (or pressure). For the first time, the actual inside causes of performance anxiety were discovered.

This is how you can create performance anxiety:

1. Believe that there is an audience made up of important people who can judge you.

2. In the "back of your mind" consider that you could fail in front of them.

3. Have a strong need to do well to avoid failure.

4. Feel unsure of yourself as to whether or not you will do well.

5. Focus on yourself.

These inside causes can result in the bodily responses associated with performance anxiety. Only then, once these bodily responses occur, can performance anxiety arise. The bodily responses could be increased heart rate, muscular tension, sweating, shaking, butterflies in the stomach area, indigestion, and the like. *If the associated bodily responses do not occur, neither will the performance anxiety.* This is because, although the "inside" causes initiate these bodily responses, both are necessary for performance anxiety to happen.

There you have it. These five causes, taken together with the associated bodily responses make up performance anxiety. If you've ever experienced performance anxiety (and most of us have on numerous occasions) this should all look familiar. After all, *you are the one who participates in the creation of these causes.* Remember, if you permit all five of these inside causes to be in your mind, then you will create performance anxiety. Regardless of how "pressure packed" a situation is, if you can avoid any one of the five inside causes, performance anxiety (pressure) will disappear!

HOW SUPER-ATHLETES DEAL WITH PRESSURE

Now that you know how we cause pressure, let's see how super-athletes try to avoid or remove those causes using the Focus Edge. Be forewarned: this is pretty tricky business. Even the superstars are vulnerable to the performance anxiety that can happen during pressure situations. They are not always successful in handling these situations. At times, they, too, succumb to the situation and experience pressure. However, more times than most, they are able to avoid the causes of performance anxiety and be successful. Let's see how they do it. (All quotes were taken from interviews by the authors with each athlete.)

WADE BOGGS (Baseball)

Wade was one of the greatest and most consistent hitters of all time. What is pressure to Wade? "I love pressure. Baseball is a team-oriented game made up of nine players, but once you get in the batter's box it is all up to you, center stage. No one else can help you. I love this situation." Wade enjoys "being on the spot." The challenge is there, but how did he keep pressure situations from turning into performance anxiety?

"I love pressure."

Wade had an incredible ability to play the game within himself. He got into a "cocoon" and blocked things out. He did this by having regular routines or rituals. For example, before a game, he ate chicken, took hundreds of ground balls, and did things like that. This pregame routine highlighted his need for consistency and predictability. It gave him something to focus on so that negative thoughts would not enter his mind. It was part of his way of avoiding uncertainty.

Within his cocoon, Wade controlled his mindset. Wade goes on to say, "I always had positive thoughts that I was going to beat the pitcher and I was going to knock in the run. If I failed, I did the very best that I could. I tried as hard as I could have. If I did succeed, it bred confidence." For Wade, either way, success or failure, there is nothing to lose.

Wade avoided performance anxiety by staying with his own goals and mental processes rather than worrying about pleasing others, which always has an element of uncertainty about it. Instead of seeing pressure situations as chances for failure, he saw them as opportunities to perform and demonstrate his skills. He had confidence in his abilities and that also helped reduce uncertainty.

JACK NICKLAUS (Golf)

"... it's just a game."

When golf legend Jack Nicklaus was asked about pressure, he asserted "Pressure doesn't mean anything to me." He went on, "Hey, it's just a game. You don't have to take it so seriously. There is more to life than the game." Nicklaus doesn't let anything consume him. "I live a life of balance and it is easy to accept failure as well as success. I do want to win at everything and I try to give everything. But if I lose after having given my best effort, then so be it. Life goes on and there will be many more days of golf." Jack never let golf become a mania. He never put all of his eggs in one basket.

Jack stayed cool by keeping things in perspective, and this takes the place of a fearful desire to avoid failure. By having a balanced life, where neither winning nor losing were the ultimate, he did not have to struggle with the strong need to avoid failure that leads so many to experience performance anxiety.

CRAIG BIGGIO (Baseball)

"... prepare for the next time, and just let it happen."

Craig is one of the best all-around second basemen to ever play the game of baseball. When he started to feel pressure because things were not going well, he let go of the negative feelings and tried to figure out the problem. "I do get nervous, but, I realize that there is no control. I just try to figure out what is happening, prepare for the next time, and just let it happen." For Craig, the problem was not outside himself. He figured out what was going on within him and built this into a preparation and not an attempt to get control.

"In tight situations, I stay with my preparation and potential. I know what I can and can't do. As a hitter, my goal is always to take what the pitcher is going to give me and adjust to the situation. In a pressure situation, with men on base," Craig said, "just bring them in. Just do it!"

Craig said that his kids had taught him a lot about dealing with pressure. "They are always there and don't care how I perform. This is particularly true for my 3-year-old and 11-month-old child." He feels unconditional acceptance from his children. That is what is important to him. There is more to life than baseball. This multitalented second baseman points to family, and particularly to his kids, for that balanced perspective that kept baseball from becoming too important. "No matter what happens, I can always return to the stability of my family. My kids don't care how I perform. I am always their daddy." Craig went on, "Nobody is perfect all of the time. In a tight situation I do get nervous but then I realize the big picture, that I do not have control and all I can do is prepare and just let things happen. I will just stay within my own potential."

Craig dealt with pressure by focusing on his family, his preparation, and his potential and let go of any need to control any outcomes that he could not control. His family was the audience of important people, but he knew they would not judge him on his performance. In addition, he stressed having "doable" goals, which increased his confidence and reduced uncertainty.

MARIO ANDRETTI (Auto Racing)

The great race car driver Mario Andretti loves pressure situations. "Without pressure, life is dull and boring." For Mario, without pressure

> **"I like pushing the edge."**

there is nothing to gain. When the pressure was on, he slowed down to reason things out. "At Indianapolis, with 250,000 people in the stands, my reasoning went like this. Car feels the same as when no one is there. This is my job. Just ignore everything else and become arrogant to the situation. This means being confident in yourself. I will not let the crowd or anyone interfere with me. When it comes to my work, I change and will step on anyone who gets in my way." Mario offered one final thought. "I always look at the glass as half-full. Pressure? I like pushing the edge. In life there are many peaks and valleys and more valleys than peaks. If you dwell in and get stuck in the valleys, it is all over. Maintain the positive and stay goal oriented."

Mario was without performance anxiety because he loved the pressure and wanted to see what he could do rather than having a need to avoid failure or satisfy others. He clearly was not concerned about pleasing others or how others judged him. He was his own man and worked hard to do what was needed to reach his goals.

Johnny Unitas (Football)

"Pressure is felt when you get overly excited ..."

Hall of Fame quarterback Johnny Unitas was Mr. Cool under pressure. He would be standing in the pocket with onrushing linemen charging him from all directions, and there he was, appearing so relaxed. It was as if he was all alone with no one else around. Like most of the super-athletes, Johnny U. understood that we put pressure on ourselves. "Pressure is felt when you get overly excited and lack knowledge of a situation. For me, I didn't put pressure on myself. I was always thinking about what I should do. Thinking about the situation knocks out excitement and emotion. Then there is no room for distractions to appear."

For Johnny, mechanical, repetitious thought could become habitual. Then you can lose attention as the mind wanders and gravitates to thoughts and images. So, keeping thoughts flexible and focused on the changing situations of the game fully occupies the mind. There is no room for feelings of pressure.

Johnny kept performance anxiety out by continuously thinking and problem solving each situation and leaving no room for any concerns about himself to appear.

Jerry West (Basketball)

"... feel determined with a quiet confidence ..."

Jerry West was a scoring machine for the Los Angeles Lakers basketball team. He was particularly cool under pressure. He was the guy the Lakers would go to in "crunch time." Jerry says, "It was easier for me during pressure situations because opponents were afraid of fouling me or making mistakes. Now this made it a lot easier for me to get to the basket and score and win the game for the team.

I would always feel determined with a quiet confidence in these pressure situations."

For Jerry, nervousness did occur before a game. "I was always nervous before a game. I owed the fans and didn't want to let them down. This was a sort of pressure but I used it." He expected to be nervous. "If the nervousness was not there, I thought something must be wrong. It was part of my ritual and I expected it." It appears that his nervousness was transformed into some kind of energy so Jerry could use it in competition.

Jerry was immune to performance anxiety because he was having fun since he felt the pressure was on his opponent. There was no fear of failure. Also, because the pressure was on his opponents, he expected them to be hesitant and timid at crunch time. This helped him avoid the uncertainty that can lead to performance anxiety.

GARY PLAYER (Golf)

The exceptional golfer, Gary Player, loved pressure. "I thrived on pressure. My focus was on winning. And if I didn't win, then I could accept adversity knowing that I did my best." Gary has a strong belief in God. He felt that his role in life was to do his duty for God. "I always had tremendous faith that God would use me as one of his servants. I felt like that I wanted to represent God." Notice that there was nothing for Gary to gain or lose. He had no illusions that he was in control. Rather, he saw his abilities as a gift. "Talent and ability are on a loan basis from God and could end anytime." Because Gary did not fill himself with importance, he could feel and enjoy the pressures of the game without these pressures being of concern to his self-image.

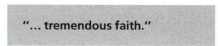

"… tremendous faith."

Gary was without performance anxiety due to his faith and belief that there was nothing for him to gain or lose. God was in control, so there was no fear of failure. Gary's belief that God's will would prevail allowed him to accept losses as part of God's plan and, therefore, not something that had to be avoided at all costs.

NANCY LOPEZ (Golf)

Nancy helped revolutionize women's golf. Her extraordinary performances brought attention to the women's game. Pressure was a constant

"… little challenges to make it fun."

companion of Nancy throughout her childhood. "I would put tremendous pressure on myself. I used to throw up before big tournaments. This is because I wanted to play real well and was not sure that I would." During this time Nancy worked closely with her father. A turning point occurred when her father became concerned and said, "Nancy, if this keeps up you are going to get an ulcer. And if this happens, you know what this will mean? You won't be able to play golf anymore." This really woke Nancy up. She knew how pressure felt, but she usually would put all of her focus on doing well.

Now something had changed. Being able to play golf became even more important than doing well. Although doing well was still important, she realized none of this would happen if she couldn't play the game. Her priorities had changed. "I loved golf, so I let go of pressure. The key to my success was my father who put no pressure on me. Instead, he encouraged my practice through creating little challenges to make it fun."

Nancy solved the problem of performance anxiety through realizing that her love for the game and having fun were both more important than doing well to avoid failure.

DEION SANDERS (Football and Baseball)

"… do the undone …"

Deion is unique. He has been able to participate in two professional sports, football and baseball. He has blazing speed and is considered one of the best defensive backs to have ever played the game. Usually, Deion took one half the field away from his opponent's passing game. No one wanted to throw to his side of the field. When he fielded a punt, he was always a threat to go all the way. And, in baseball, Deion was a very consistent base stealer. Overall, Deion was an exceptional athlete who could do many things at a very high level of performance. What is pressure to Deion?

"My whole life has been dealing with pressure. Ever since I was six years old, people expected more of me than others. I am used to these expectations." So, for Deion, pressure is nothing new. He expects it. But notice here! These expectations meant that people believed he was good and wanted more from him than others. This is quite different from expectations that mean "we need you to do well and not let us down."

Deion added, "The most important thing … keep pressure from bothering you … know yourself and play within yourself. I know my limits. But within those limits, I have no limits. I want to do what has never been done before. To be creative, to do the undone, to show the unseen."

Deion coped with performance anxiety through focusing on the step-by-step process of a task and blocking out any thoughts about possible failure. He replaced such thoughts with positive visualizations of the outcome. He has great confidence in his ability to reach his "doable" goals to "… be creative, to do the undone, to show the unseen." Because he was confident that he had the ability to reach these goals, he avoided uncertainty.

Don Garlits (Auto Racing)

Don "Big Daddy" Garlits was a superstar drag racer. He is credited with the development of the rear engine dragster. He was both super-racer and super-mechanic. "Big Daddy" admits there was pressure:

"… take a little at a time."

I had a lot of respect for fear but I was not afraid of it. I was not afraid because I built the cars myself. But if I ever started thinking that I was going to lose a race that I had to win, the minute that the thought that I might lose came into my mind, I completely blanked it out and swept it right out of there. I was not going to lose and I will not think about losing. Then I would immediately start concentrating on and imagining after the race. I saw myself in the victory circle, the trophy presentation, the photographers standing around me who might be asking me questions and things like that.

Don remembers one time when there was tremendous pressure to fix a car in time to enter a big race:

To get this done in time looked impossible to a lot of people. But we did it! How did we do it? I told the boys that we just needed to take a little at a time. We had torches, tools, and expertise. Each man had his own job to do. Each took his time to make sure it was done right and then moved on to the next thing. We never looked at the whole project. Instead of not seeing the trees for the forest, we got right into the forest and picked each tree. We said, "Yeah, this is a maple, this is an ash," and so on. This is how we got it done. We won the race and set a new record at 252 miles per hour.

Overall, "Big Daddy" is pointing out that you need to focus on the step-by-step process and not the final result and how hard it might be to get there.

Don coped with performance anxiety through focusing on the step-by-step process of a task. This allowed him to focus on the positive and lock out any negative thoughts that could lead to performance anxiety (like avoiding failure). He replaced such thoughts with detailed positive visualizations of the outcome. He also had confidence in his abilities, and because he always stayed within the limits of his abilities, he was able to avoid uncertainty.

STEVE KINER (Football)

> "... don't let [performance] anxiety move from your body up to your head."

All-Pro Steve Kiner, inductee into the College Football Hall of Fame and winner of the Dick Butkus award for outstanding linebacker in the NFL, loved impact. He really enjoyed hitting people. "It was during those times when the pressure was on that I was at my best. The adrenaline was flowing. It was at this time that I felt most alive! In the moment, anticipating and waiting." In Steve's view, pressure meant opportunity, the opportunity to meet a challenge.

When Steve Kiner first went to the pros his pregame jitters were very intense. "I found myself trembling and shaking all over. I would get really sick to my stomach and vomit just before a game. It was like I couldn't stop this response." The intensity of the situation overwhelmed him, but let's listen further to Steve: "Eventually I learned to use this response. I used all this nervousness as part of my pregame ritual. This became part of getting ready and building up my intensity." He adds, "The important thing is, don't let anxiety move from your body up to your head." Feel it. Don't start thinking about it! "The feeling kept me in the moment and that is where all the energy is." The bottom line is being able to stay in the moment. When you start anxious thinking (as in the five inside causes of performance anxiety, on page 110), you lose the moment. Do you see what Steve did here? He accepted the stress and the pressure and changed them into assets.

Steve nipped performance anxiety in the bud. He used its energy through not letting the initial physical feelings move up into the head with thoughts and concerns about failure.

JOAN BENOIT (Track)

> "... decide to have faith in the past ..."

Joan Benoit is one of the greatest distance runners of all time. For Joan, pressure meant being concerned about others. "Pressure is carrying the expectations of others in order to have their respect and not necessarily to impress them." She emphasized the importance of staying within yourself. Joan could not control the expectations of others. Before each race, she felt these expectations for her as being either a favorite or an underdog. "I liked coming into a race as an underdog. Then there was nothing to lose. But when I felt that I was the favorite, I would decide to have faith in the past and focus on my performance history, my past races. I blocked out the other things."

Joan avoided performance anxiety through focusing on positive past performances (like successful races and training sessions) and blocking out concerns about the expectations of others.

Ted Williams (Baseball)

Ted is considered by many to be the greatest hitter of all time. He was a master of the game, always perfecting. Ted focused on the little things that would continue to make him a better hitter.

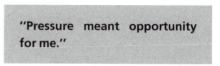

"Pressure meant opportunity for me."

This built the confidence that would be with him in pressure situations and help remove any uncertainty. "I liked it when men were on base. Pressure meant opportunity for me." For Ted, pressure situations were test situations. They enabled him to express all the hard work that he had put into his preparation. "These situations were a challenge to me because I knew what I could do." The audience (the fans) had a different meaning for Ted. He expected them to respond to his greatness. If they didn't, then "the hell with them."

Ted reduced performance anxiety by focusing on perfecting his skills and testing them in tight situations. Pressure situations were not times when he felt others might judge him. Rather, he demanded their admiration. Overall, a pressure situation was a test situation, rather than a survival issue in which one must avoid failure. In those situations Ted simply "tested" himself.

Gordie Howe (Hockey)

Gordie was one of hockey's most prolific scorers. Pressure did not exist for him. "I never felt fear during a game. Before a game I would get very excited, not anxious. And then when

"It is important not to let yourself get psyched out by others."

the puck was dropped and the game began, even that went away. I never knew pressure was there until after the game was over."

What about distractions? "I could hear the sound of the crowd and my name but no details. It is important not to let yourself get psyched out by others, like trash talking and things like that." Although he had good peripheral vision, Gordie was not distracted by anything that went on beyond the ice. In the back of his mind was always the one overriding goal, "Score one goal every third game. This was a very doable goal for me so I never worried."

Gordie did not have performance anxiety. The crowd existed only as a muffled sound in the background. For him, all that was important were his very "doable" goals. Because he had such confidence in his abilities, "doable" goals (like "score a goal every three games") allowed him to avoid uncertainty. If he had a scoring "slump," he could renew his confidence in his abilities by something as simple as scoring a goal in practice.

JEFF BAGWELL (Baseball)

"think... 'this is fun'... a chance to entertain people."

Jeff was an exceptional long ball hitter and RBI guy. He was one of baseball's superstars. In pressure situations he experienced more of an adrenaline rush than a feeling of pressure.

It's more excitement than anxiety. I am focused more on making something happen. This is instead of trying to avoid something. If I am in a tight situation and facing a great pitcher, I think "This is fun. This is what the fans want to see." These are the best moments of the game. I am given a chance to entertain people. Pressure situations are the fun part of the game. They are opportunities. Baseball is just a game but it is a lot of fun.

Jeff avoided performance anxiety by enjoying being a performer. He liked being "on stage." Instead of looking at pressure situations as opportunities to be judged, Jeff viewed them as opportunities to entertain the audience. It was as if a part of him was up in the stands enjoying the game. The audience was there to have fun, and he owed his best to help them enjoy themselves.

JEARL MILES (Track)

"... just believe that whatever is going to happen is going to happen."

Jearl is a 1988 and 1992 Olympian and 1993 World Champion. She has been one of America's finest middle-distance runners for quite some time.

Her coach, J. J. Clark is most impressed with her cool demeanor under pressure. He said, "I will never forget the time that we were on a bus going to one of the biggest meets of the year. There she was, real relaxed, painting her fingernails." When asked about this she replied, "I can't lose since I will always have my family and close friends with me." She emphasized that the key to her success is having this really significant support system. A supportive, caring, and nurturing family provided the context in which to excel. People outside this system do not really matter that much. In this way, the expectations and judgments of large, impersonal crowds were of no consequence.

What is pressure for Jearl? "I just believe that whatever is going to happen is going to happen. So, I just do what I can do like train hard and prepare. Then, during pressure situations, I simply do what I have prepared to do. I stay with my plan and I focus on executing it." Although Jearl could experience the pressure situation, the feeling of pressure was absent.

Jearl was without performance anxiety because of an ability to let go of those things that she had no control over. Most importantly, she had a caring, nonjudgmental audience. In addition, she had "doable" goals: preparing and following her plan. She knew she could do these two things so there was little uncertainty for her.

Mark Price (Basketball)

Mark was a great player for the Cleveland Cavaliers and later the Orlando Magic. At one time he was the most accurate free-throw shooter in NBA history. Mark said:

> "... be the so-called goat for a chance to be a hero."

I am not afraid of pressure. People remember the five or ten shots that Michael Jordan made at the end of a game to win and they don't remember the fifty he missed. If you calculate it, the chance of hitting a shot at the end of a game is not very high. Some guys are afraid to take that chance. They don't want to be a hero unless there is a 100% chance and they don't want to take any chance of being the goat. I am willing to be the so-called goat for a chance to be a hero. Getting the ball in "crunch time" is exciting and challenging. I am thinking, "Hey, I can make it and I am going to take it. If I don't make it, well at least I gave myself a chance."

Mark slipped past performance anxiety through believing there is nothing to lose. He knew that the chances and expectations of making that last shot were low and, even should he miss, it would easily be forgotten. Since people would easily forget the missed shots, he was not worried about being judged. Thus there was no fear of failure and no performance anxiety.

KAREN BLISS LIVINGSTON (Cycling)

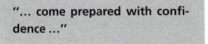

"... come prepared with confidence ..."

Super cyclist **Karen Bliss Livingston** was named U.S. Cycling Athlete of the Year in 1997. Karen put great emphasis on training and her overall preparation for a race.

> When I feel prepared and come to the start of a race with confidence, the pressure does not bother me one bit. But if I come to the starting line knowing I have not prepared then I really feel the pressure. When I come prepared with confidence, I like the fact that my teammates expect me to win. I like the feeling that they can count on me. Being prepared means a long training period.

Karen avoided performance anxiety by completing her doable goal of being prepared. This helped reduce the uncertainty of whether or not she could be successful.

CHARLIE TRIPPI (Football)

"I honestly didn't know what pressure was. It was too much fun."

Charlie Trippi, the outstanding triple-threat back of the old Chicago Cardinals and one of the University of Georgia's greatest all-time football players, really appreciated the game. It allowed him to stay out of the coal mines. For Charlie, everything about the game was fun. In pressure situations, he felt no need to prove himself. He wanted to give to the fans and give them a good show and what they paid for. In Charlie's own words, "I always expected to win. But if I lost, I would feel bad but knew that some days I am not going to win. I always loved the big game. I honestly didn't know what pressure was. It was too much fun."

Charlie couldn't relate to performance anxiety. He had perspective. The alternative to playing the game was a difficult and hard life. So the game was fun.

RAY NITSCHKE (Football)

Ray was a member of Vince Lombardi's legendary Green Bay Packer teams and, arguably, one of the greatest linebackers of all time. Ray said:

> "... reckless abandonment, like there was no tomorrow."

I looked for tight situations. I thrived on them. I wanted to be there when the game was on the line. When you have done something for a period of time, you have confidence and there is no pressure. Yes, there was fear but no pressure. I knew everyone was watching, but didn't hear them and didn't want to fall on my face. But I was confident. I worked hard and I always felt ready for anything. The game was my passion. I lived it. I played with reckless abandonment, like there was no tomorrow. I was fiercely competitive and aggressive. This all came from my mother and father dying when I was young.

Ray left no room for performance anxiety. He was totally involved with the intensity of the momentary situation. His thorough preparation left him confident, removing any doubts about what he was able to do.

GETTING RID OF YOUR
PERFORMANCE ANXIETY

Do you remember the five "inside" causes of performance anxiety (page 110)? How do these super-athletes use the Focus Edge to remove them? Let's take a little closer look. Remember: avoiding even one of the five causes makes it impossible for performance anxiety to occur.

1. Believe there is an audience made up of important people who can judge you.

Boggs, Andretti, Sanders, Benoit, and Miles were not threatened by the crowd. One way they did this was by concentrating on their own, doable goals. This is one way to block out the crowd. Others, like Jeff Bagwell, cast the audience in a positive light and saw them as supportive or providing the athlete with an opportunity to entertain them. Remember, even if others expect you to perform well, there is no pressure as long as you agree with them and also expect to perform well. That is why the thorough preparation that is characteristic of super-athletes is so helpful. It breeds confidence and they expect themselves to perform well.

2. In the "back of your mind" consider that you could fail in front of them.

This cause has to do with focusing on the possibility of something going wrong. This could be a negative image or a thought about a negative outcome. Garlits, Kiner, and Benoit mentioned the use of thought control. Garlits would create the imagery of the future through detailed seeing of the way he wanted things to turn out. Benoit pulled images of successful competitions and training from the past. Kiner simply kept feelings from rising into his head and becoming thoughts about negative possibilities.

3. Focus on yourself.

This cause centers on your preoccupation with yourself. You see the eyes of others as if they were cameras. You are on stage! You are not looking at them, but they are looking at you. You see this audience as a blur. Why? Because your focus and main concern is yourself. A frequent thought might be "How am I doing?" Even though Bagwell felt "on stage," he experienced this audience as an opportunity to "show off" rather than be judged. Focus is on others and not self. Unitas and others point out how keeping your mind filled with thoughts about problem-solving your goals allows no room for thoughts about self to enter. Still others, like Ray Nitschke, fill the space through total involvement in the present situation. The game situation unfolding in front of you becomes all that exists. Self disappears. There is just so much space in your mind. You can either fill it with whatever you wish or permit a flood of unwanted, anxious thoughts to come in.

4. Have a strong need to do well to avoid failure.

This cause provides the main fuel for performance anxiety. It is the strong need to avoid failure. Barry Larkin, superstar of the Cincinnati Reds, emphasized to us how the fear of failure paralyzes the performance of so many young athletes. When something becomes too important, the strong desire to avoid losing it can easily turn into anxiety. Nicklaus, Trippi, and Player all had perspective. They did not take things too seriously. For them, there was more to life than the results of a game. There is God, family, and other interests. The stronger these other interests are, the less important the game has to become. Still another way to knock out the feeling of pressure is to change the goal. Change from a desire to avoid failure to a positive goal like entertaining people or giving yourself a chance to be a hero or doing your best. West and Lopez emphasized having fun.

5. Feel unsure of yourself as to whether or not you will do well.

This cause relates to uncertainty and lack of confidence. You cannot have anxiety without uncertainty. If you choose goals that you have little or no control over, you will be vulnerable to performance anxiety. Although many of the super-athletes say that they are not sure how things are going to turn out, they all feel certain about what they can do. Even though they are not sure whether they will win or not, they are all confident of their abilities. "I'd just come off a very difficult year," said Michael Jordan. "I had to fight the Bulls just to get back on the floor after I broke my foot. You could say I was getting my business education. I've never been afraid to assert myself on or off the court." Williams, Boggs, Biggio, Andretti, and others all underscored the importance of playing the game within yourself and staying with your goals. "I came to feel," said Doug Rogers, "that not only could I be champion, but I must." As Gordie Howe points out, "Make sure that you have goals you believe are doable." That brings confidence and takes away uncertainty. Thorough preparation is another way that many super-athletes reduce uncertainty.

Now we have seen how individual super-athletes respond to pressure and how they defeat performance anxiety. Although each has his/her own way of avoiding performance anxiety, what is it that they share in common? What is an effective mindset that would represent all these super-athletes? Because this mindset is general, it can be learned and applied by anyone and everyone involved in pressure situations. We can call this the Focus Edge mindset to deal with pressure!

THE FOCUS EDGE FORMULA FOR DEALING WITH PRESSURE

When the pressure is on, you do have a choice as to how you respond, but that is easier said than done. Most of the time things happen too quickly. You react and choice goes out the window. To be effective in reducing performance anxiety, you must already have the appropriate *mindset*. This mindset must either be a "natural" part of your personality or it needs to be learned ahead of time. Super-athletes bring this mindset to the table. When a pressure situation occurs, they most often respond optimally.

Let's take some examples of pressure situations in nonathletic situations. Hitting an oil slick and losing control of your car, being in the midst of a tornado, escaping a fire that breaks out in a theater, and piloting a plane that is losing fuel can all present themselves as a crisis. Notice how different people's reactions can be to these situations. You may experience no choices and no anxiety with your car out of control. There is nothing to do or that can be done. Being in the presence of a tornado might present choices such as, "Should I try to outrun the tornado?" (usually a bad choice) or "Should I get to the nearest ditch?" In a theater, fire choices may be, "Should I rush to the nearest exit or should I calmly walk outside?" What should you do? Uncertainty may engulf you. In these situations you can feel panic or full-blown anxiety. Now, piloting a plane that is losing fuel can be quite different. In this situation, you probably know what needs to be done. You're familiar with the instruments and are probably looking for an emergency landing area. You may be busy problem solving. You probably know what you can and can't do. Uncertainty is absent and there may be no anxiety! The well-trained pilot and the super-athlete come prepared for the situation. Performance anxiety is unlikely.

Don't become confused by these examples. *Situations do not cause anxiety.* That comes from our responses to the situations. However, some situations may trigger anxiety more easily than others. The fact is you could respond to any of the above examples either with or without anxiety. It all depends on the mindset you bring to the situation. For example, if the pilot was focused on what was going to happen to him or her, something that was not under the pilot's control, uncertainty could arise, and with it, anxiety. *What is important is that you have an effective mindset in the midst of a crisis or pressure situation.* Super-athletes are prepared. Are you? We will now turn to the mindset that is the super-athlete's solution for how to handle pressure.

What is this calm midst the storm? Here is one super-athlete's description: "It's so high energy. Everything is energized. Yet everything is narrowed to one goal and my focus goes toward that. It's a powerful situation. It's like you are driving around a tight corner and you see a diesel coming at you. You either find an escape route or you go over the cliff. I don't hear the crowd. It is like whatever senses you do not need to be on turn off." This description underscores the importance of focus. *Performance anxiety is impossible when there is effective concentration.* Notice the energy that is available when there is pressure. The uncertainty of the situation produces it. Super-athletes call it an adrenaline rush. There is a challenge and you feel capable, but if, for a moment, you focus on the uncertainty of your performance, that same energy can be squandered in the expression of performance anxiety. There are many traps! So how can we avoid these traps?

We want to make the super-athlete solution to dealing with pressure situations as simple as we can. In order to do this, let's briefly look again at the different types of goals. If I'm a batter I might say, "I want to get a hit." That is a *result goal.* The hit is a result of the batter performing a certain process (watching the pitch, deciding whether and where and when and how to swing). The hit is a "result" of the process and other factors such as where fielders are positioned, the wind, etc. Therefore, getting a hit is a positive *approach result goal.* Another type of *result goal* is an *avoidance goal*—"I want to avoid striking out." It's also a result, but one that the player sees as negative and wants to avoid.

Notice that *result goals are not really under a person's control.* A batter can make a good swing and not get a hit. A pitcher makes a great pitch that is too hard to hit. A fielder might make a great play. The wind may be blowing in and hold a ball up for a fielder. All of these factors are out of the hitter's control and may keep the hitter from achieving the result goal of getting a hit. Athletes often set *performance goals* to help them reach their result goals. *Performance goals are specific physical and mental actions athletes can take to help reach result goals.* For example, hitting the ball hard can be a performance goal for a batter. Hitting the ball hard can help a batter meet his result goal of getting a hit. *Athletes have more control over performance goals*—it is easier to hit the ball hard than it is to get a hit. It is even easier to just make contact than it is to hit a ball hard. It is even easier to make an optimal swing than it is to just make contact with a pitch.

Now let's pull this Focus Edge mindset together. What are the characteristics that make it so effective in avoiding performance anxiety? For reducing pressure, super-athletes agree on three factors:

1. a positive general goal as motivation,

2. a controllable performance goal to bolster confidence, and

3. concentration on the moment-to-moment process of what they are doing.

1. **Motivation: Choose a positive general goal.** With this goal there are no boundaries. The sky is the limit. *Desire rather than fear drives you.* Examples would be entertain the crowd, have fun, challenge yourself, and appreciate the opportunity you have to show what you can do. There is nothing to lose. During "crunch time," you want to be out there. You want the opportunity to be the hero. Even if it means being the goat, you want the opportunity to be the one. Can you see how each of the above examples is positive? Each of the above goals is something that you can direct your energy toward achieving as opposed to something you are trying to avoid (like losing, failing, being embarrassed, being judged, etc.).

2. **Confidence: Select a specific ability-related performance goal.** This goal must be something that you know is "doable" for you, *something over which you have control.* Examples would be make your optimal swing through the strike zone, study film to become well acquainted with the defense you are going to face on Sunday, go through a very specific ritual at the free-throw line before taking your shot, or go through a very specific warm-up before your race. Can you see how each of the above goals is "doable," meaning it is under the control of the athlete? Regardless of what any other player or coach does, an athlete can do a specific warm-up or carry out a specific ritual at the free-throw line or study film. Having these types of goals helps remove uncertainty, because they are under your control.

3. **Concentration: Focus on the process.** *Stay in touch with the moment-to-moment process* because over-concern with results can get you in

trouble. Examples would be a golfer getting the feel of the club in her hands, an outfielder noticing the direction of the wind before a pitch, or a running back imagining himself hitting a hole just before the snap of the ball. Do you see what these goals have in common? They all revolve around the moment-to-moment process athletes go through while actually competing. By focusing on the moment-to-moment process, it is easier to keep distracting thoughts out of one's mind.

Watch the *pitfalls*! Here are some examples. *You want to win so you can avoid being labeled a loser.* Sorry. Although wanting to win sounds positive, look what is hidden behind it: the fear of being a loser. This is not a positive general goal. It is negative. What about the performance goal of *showing others what you can do*? The trap here is "show others." Although you are focused on your ability, you have no control over whether or not your ability will be appreciated by others. Rather, you need to be focused on having the opportunity to "show others."

Another goal may be to *try hard to stay focused and concentrated.* The key word here is "try." When you try, you can create tension. Then with each effort to remain concentrated, you lose focus at that moment. Focus should not be effortful and rigid. It needs to be flowing and effortless while being supported by confidence and fearlessness.

This is it! *Have a general goal that is positive, a performance goal that relates to your abilities, and focus on the process of what you are doing.* With these three, pressure cannot exist. This is how super-athletes perform under pressure. With this Focus Edge mindset, you can now help both yourself as well as others when there is difficulty in handling the pressures of life.

APPLYING THE FOCUS EDGE MINDSET

You have been shown how to reduce the pressure of *performance anxiety*. You may now be wondering how you can use this information to help others. Whether you are a coach, teacher, manager, consultant, executive, or parent, you will want to know how to apply this solution. To answer the question of how, we'll draw from some of our experiences as professional sports consultants.

Remember Barry Larkin saying:

> The big problem with many of the young kids in this game is they fear failure. The pressure gets to them. When I am hitting, the pressure is always on the pitcher. I will never put pressure on myself. After all, in this game, I'm likely to fail seven out of ten times at bat. So why fear failure? I always put pressure outside myself. If I'm hitting in a tight situation, I feel the pitcher is in trouble. He has the pressure to get me out.[1]

Matt Williams agreed, "As a hitter, the pressure is really on the pitcher. I could stand up there and do nothing and he could still walk me. The pressure is not on me. This may sound strange, but I could even enjoy striking out with the bases loaded. I just want to be there and have the opportunity."[2]

In our consulting work, we use this idea of turning pressure around and putting it on the opposition. In short, we *reverse the pressure*. Over the years we've seen how many athletes and even entire teams were more successful when cast in the "bad guy" role or the role of a "spoiler."

Think about this for a moment. What happens when you enjoy seeing yourself as the bad guy or spoiler? It can be lots of fun and it's a positive goal you can strive to reach. Some of us remember the old Oakland Raiders on the road. They wore their black and silver uniforms. They were the bad guys and could ruin a Sunday afternoon for the home folks, and they loved doing it! It's no coincidence that they had an excellent road-winning record.

A *spoiler* can use surprise as a tool. At one point we were working with the San Francisco 49ers. They were preparing to play their hated rivals, the LA Rams. We suggested to the coaching staff that they adopt the mindset of having fun. One way to do this was to have the team see themselves in the role of spoilers and surprise the Rams and their fans with a big effort, while not being concerned about results. Focus was to be on the process (a performance goal) and not the results. The goal was to make a big effort (a "doable goal" over which the 49er players had control) and see what might happen.

The Rams had a winning streak going and we could upset them. It would be particularly sweet because it was on the road, in their "backyard" and in front of their fans. The coaching staff "implanted" the spoiler mindset early in the week and just prior to kickoff. This was done in team meetings and meetings of the coaching staff and as continuous reminders on the practice field. *The result was a big upset and blowout of the Rams.*

If the 49ers were to concentrate on results (such as the score), there would be significant uncertainty about the outcome. However, by choosing a doable goal like making a big effort, the uncertainty was removed because they knew they could do that. It was under their control. Also, their doable goal took the place of avoiding failure (losing) and removed the audience (crowd) as potential judges. There was *little to lose* but lots to gain—the fun of ruining the day for the Rams and their fans.

We used the spoiler mindset to reverse pressure on another occasion as well. We were consulting with the University of Florida Gators football team. It was prior to their big game in Jacksonville, Florida, with the University of Georgia Bulldogs. This game is a "border war" between the two states. None of their previous games seemed any bigger than this one. The Gators had a chance to win the SEC championship for the first time in history if they won the game. This was a pressure situation! At first their attitude was one in which they felt a need to try as hard as possible to keep from losing this game as they had in recent years. We consulted with the coaching staff, and we agreed that a different attitude was needed. It was not from lack of effort that they had not been able to beat Georgia in recent years.

The goal of the mindset we helped the coaching staff develop for the team included *having fun and focusing on making a big effort that will mount from quarter to quarter.* The Florida players were simply to stay with this process of increasing their effort every quarter. They were to ignore any concerns about results, such as score, first downs, etc. The players knew that their fans were used to seeing the Gators roll over, play dead, and let the hated "Dawgs" push them around and take charge.

But now something had changed. No longer was there the feeling of "My God, we can't let this happen again." In its place and in the back of their minds was the *spoiler role,* "Wouldn't it be funny if we surprised all those people and shocked them with a relentless, big, mounting effort from start to finish, regardless of the score!" Nothing more was said about winning or the need to win. The result was a big Gator victory and their first ever SEC title.

Once again, the goal selected was doable. The Gators were capable of controlling their effort, increasing it every quarter. This removed uncertainty about how they would do. If they had focused on the score, there could have been considerable uncertainty. And again, there was nothing to lose but lots to gain in this situation. They wanted to surprise the huge crowd by doing something they were certain they could do. It was Georgia that would feel the pressure of trying to avoid losing their recent dominance in this game.

When you see yourself as a *spoiler,* it's then up to the opposition to prevent you from spoiling their party. *The pressure is off of you and on them!* It is up to them to try and keep the unthinkable from happening. For the opposition, an avoidance goal as well as an uncertain expectation can easily arise. You know what that means. When you really want to avoid something very badly (like losing) and feel shaky (uncertain) about whether you can do it, performance anxiety is the likely result. *That is pressure, and it is on the other team.*

While consulting with the San Francisco Giants, we designed groups for pinch hitters and relief pitchers to deal with pressure situations. These were athletes with limited opportunities. Whenever they had an opportunity, there was often the feeling that they had to make it count because they never knew when they would get another chance. As one relief pitcher put it, "If I give up the winning run tonight, it may be days before I can take the mound again and erase that. If they would make me their 'stopper,' then the anxiety would go because I would know my role and where I stood. I could count on being back out there on the mound soon, whether or not I fail this time. The uncertainty would be taken away."

Similarly, a pinch hitter complained about how hard it was to get in the flow of the game. Each at bat became too important. He said, "I need to feel I am a role player like 'the man of the bench' or 'Mr. Clutch.' Otherwise I am always trying to prove myself."

One of these hitters was **Joel Youngblood**. At the time, Joel was struggling while batting in the low .200s. Each at bat seemed crucial to him. We worked with Joel and helped him open up his perspective. *He discovered more important things in his life than baseball.* These included things like family and spiritual concerns. We also taught Joel *how to observe himself without judgment.* He became aware of how he was creating his own pressure. He sometimes would laugh and find this humorous, a sign that he had stopped judging himself so harshly. He would say, "This is crazy. I don't need to keep doing this to myself. I just need to loosen up and go out and enjoy the game and see what happens."

The performance goal for Joel became simply to make his *optimal swing through the strike zone.* This he could do with certainty because he was in control of how he made his swing. This was a process and not a result, like getting a hit or even hitting the ball hard or driving the ball. The result of all this was that Joel became the Giants' second leading hitter by the end of the season and eventually one of the National League's premier pinch hitters.

Note how Joel was able to defeat pressure. Adopting a *performance goal* of making his optimal swing through the strike zone removed lots of uncertainty. Joel knew he could do this. He had done it many times in the past. It was something over which he had control. Uncertainty was removed and his goal was no longer to avoid failure—instead it was positive. If others judged him, it no longer mattered as much because he had developed a much *larger perspective.*

Mark Davis was a relief pitcher for the Giants and later the San Diego Padres. When we first met Mark, he was feeling a great deal of pressure in his role. He remarked, "When I start, I feel less pressure than when I relieve. As a starter, I feel that I win or lose the game myself. It's up to me and I don't feel like I'm letting others down like when I blow a save opportunity." This was in stark contrast to another reliever, **Jim Gott**, who felt more pressure in starting a game because it was all up to him and less pressure when he relieved because he could lose himself and feel more a part of the team. His success and failures were not as personal. *Notice how subtle these differences in meaning are but what a great difference they can make in the feelings of pressure.* This underscores the importance of getting to know in-depth the person you are trying to help. It is only then that an optimal solution can be applied.

Behind Mark's pressure was a need to feel secure. He felt baseball was all he could do. Additionally, his definition of success in the game depended a lot on how he was viewed by others. More than anything, he wanted to prove himself to others, particularly his manager. This would mean being given more opportunities to succeed and eventually becoming secure in the game. When he was pitching, errors by his own fielders did not bother him. It was those fluke hits that should have never fallen in that really upset him. He believed those hits would be seen by others as his fault.

This was the case even when Mark knew he had thrown a good pitch. It was as if Mark was always on stage and in the spotlight. From the mound and out of the corner of his eye he was apt to see the manager's reaction—like taking one step up in the dugout. To him, this could mean he was about to be pulled.

Mark needed to *let go and play the game within himself.* We discussed with him that, as a pitcher, it was sometimes not even necessary to see the hitter. *Focus should only be on the catcher's glove and throwing to it.* It was as if the pitcher and catcher were just working back and forth playing catch. This enabled Mark to stay in the moment and not let his mind wander to possible negative outcomes.

We also worked with his general goal. We talked about his interests and abilities as well as other things he could do in his life. *He realized that he had choices other than baseball.* In a way he found that he had nothing to lose because he had other things that he could fall back on. Now he could just go out and play with abandonment and enjoy the game. The game did not have to be such a serious, life-and-death matter to him.

For a *positive performance goal* we gave Mark's very active mind something to work on. He was to use his imagination and see himself as a surgeon who was a specialist who knew how to carve up the corners of the plate. With this goal, instead of pressure, pitching jams became opportunities and a *challenge.* The goal was to use his expertise and strengths to see what he could do. All this became part of Mark's Focus Edge mindset. Above all else he was to *keep things simple.*

Here was Mark's response to the Focus Edge mindset. "For the first time in my life I am pitching relaxed and with the right attitude. I am no longer thinking about the hitter. I just think about what I want to do and throw to the glove. When I first come in to pitch, I think 'What is the worst thing that could happen? A home run. And also what are the chances that this person will get a hit off of me? Pretty low since .300 is a great year.' All this stuff is unlikely, so I just put it out of my mind and go out and pitch. And if I get hit, I can't help it as long as I make my pitches."[3] The result of using this Focus Edge mindset was a year-ending 2.99 earned run average with 90 strikeouts to go with only 34 walks as one of the Giants' top relievers. Mark went on to win the Cy Young award while setting the save record with the San Diego Padres.

Mark is a rather dramatic example of what can happen when an athlete gets it "all together." He gained *perspective* on what part baseball really played in his life, and this left him with a strong feeling of *nothing to lose.* He had a new way to look at "failure" and as a result no longer had such a strong need to avoid it. His *performance goals*—throwing to the catcher's glove and "cutting up the corners"—were both positive and helped him remove negative goals, like avoiding failure.

Our final example deals with our work with **Tommy Morrison**, who at the time was ranked as one of the top heavyweight fighters in the world. He was about to face **George Foreman** for the heavyweight championship. This was a huge fight with a lot riding on it. Tommy's trainer emphasized the importance of staying out of range of George's powerful punches. Foreman's knockout-to-fight ratio was incredible. On the flip side, although Tommy was a very heavy hitter himself, it might be futile to try and knock George out. Hitting George has been likened to hitting a giant redwood tree.

One of the issues during Tommy's training camp was getting Tommy to relax and fight a "smart" fight against Foreman. However, in some previous fights and in training sessions, relaxing seemed to lower the number of punches Tommy threw and caused him to let his guard down, opening him up to disaster. One of his biggest worries was that if he unleashed a continuous flurry of punches and didn't knock out his opponent, he would then get tired and get knocked out himself. In his most recent fights, Tommy had been holding back out of fear of getting tired and, as a result, not utilizing his power and speed as he should have.

Another of Tommy's biggest fears was getting beaten badly and being embarrassed. He felt he had to avoid being embarrassed at all costs. How he looked to others in the ring was important to him. In front of a supportive home crowd, the worry was even more intense, because these were the people in front of whom he could not bear to look bad.

We worked with Tommy on *how to use the crowd instead of becoming concerned about being judged by it.* We talked about using the crowd's energy like a battery. His trainer added that he could visualize sucking the energy of the crowd through a straw. Tommy was to focus on the cheering of the crowd, their energy, but not their expectations. Next, we showed him a way to *stay in the moment* and not lose his attention. We had him feel himself looking through his eyes. Tommy responded, "This feels good!

I feel strong, like nothing can touch me." This was quite different from performance anxiety, where he felt as if all eyes were looking at him.

In a previous fight, Tommy's goal was to get that good feeling of landing punches. However, when he started missing his punches, disappointment set in and his punch output dropped. As he missed, he started to lose confidence and uncertainty set in. The result was *performance anxiety.* He tried to avoid looking bad by throwing fewer punches. He started being overly cautious. What he needed was a different goal, one that he had control over. Note that once he threw his punches, he had no control over where or if they landed. He also needed *a goal that let him stay within himself.*

What we suggested was that Tommy see himself as the "operator of his fighting machinery." Such a goal was simply to throw his punches and create flurries. We suggested that he aim his punches to land but not expect them to. We also suggested that he adopt the following theme: *the more he missed, the hungrier he would get and his punch output would increase instead of decrease.* The net result of this mental work was Tommy demonstrating an entirely new dimension in his fight game. Instead of his typical "slug it out" style, he paced himself and fought brilliantly in defeating George Foreman for the heavyweight championship.

Notice how Tommy was able to avoid his worries about being judged by the audience, especially his home fans who were so important to him. Instead of viewing them as potential judges, he learned to see them as a *source of energy* (like a battery) for his fighting. He also was able to avoid this negative-type thinking by focusing on his positive goal—"operating" his "fighting machinery." He knew the machinery could aim punches. He knew the machinery could increase its output if his punches missed. He knew these things because he was in control of them. With this new goal, uncertainty was reduced and he was able to focus on his fighting instead of the crowd.

SUMMARY

What have we learned from the super-athletes about the Focus Edge? How can you stay out of the trap of *performance anxiety*? Remember the Focus Edge mindset formula. For *motivation,* have a general positive result goal; for *confidence,* set a performance goal that relates to your abilities, and for *concentration,* be focused on the on-going process itself. Let's see if we can simplify the Focus Edge mindset solution to performance anxiety even further.

First of all, whatever you do, make sure it is what you *love* to do. It needs to be enjoyable, fun, or a passion, and this should require that you have the *ability* for it as well as an *interest*. This is your *positive general goal*. Next, when you set your goals for your activities, make sure they are something you know *how* to do and *can* do. There should be no doubt here. It's more than just a belief. It should be something you feel you have already proven to yourself. Your goal is simply to express what you already know you can do. Let the outcome happen in whatever way it does. Outcome is not your concern.

The final thing to remember might be the most important. It has to do with focus or *concentration on the moment-to-moment process*. Without focus, it matters little what your goals are. Performance will suffer. *The one thing required for optimal performance is that you are present to what you are doing.* Without this type of presence, you might find a ball stuck in your ear or your car sliding into a wall at 200 miles per hour. Accidents do happen, and they are encouraged when you become oblivious to what is happening at the moment.

Focus! The legendary quarterback Y. A. Tittle was not aware of pass rushers. He was too busy looking for receivers. Exceptional hitter, Hal McCrae, never paid attention to the situation. In the batter's box he did not concern himself with the score, the inning, people on base, or things like that. "All I focused on was what was most important for me to do right now to be successful. Like see the ball! Just deal with this moment individually and not situationally." Hall of Famer Alan Trammel was so focused that the fans became like a mirage in the background. Finally, former world record holder, Jim Ryun, was no stranger to pressure. "I always focused on what I was trying to achieve. That was the warm-up, the thought, the preparation, and all that. I just blocked out the 'what ifs'—what if I do poorly and things like that. If you allow outside circumstances to come in, you add pressure. Focus is essential!"

There you have it: the Focus Edge mindset formula for dealing with pressure situations. They need not be a problem for you any more, but do get to know *your* pressure. If you feel performance anxiety, don't try to stop it. This resistance only serves to strengthen it. Instead, welcome it and accept it. Say to yourself, "Ah. There's that performance anxiety. Now I can look at it and learn how I stirred it up."

Don't waste your energy fighting pressure and performance anxiety or talking to yourself, saying things like "What's wrong now? I shouldn't be feeling like this." Recognize pressure and admit to it. Then you can turn your attention to your positive performance goal and allow those feelings of performance anxiety to recede into the background and provide further energy for the fulfillment of your goal. Better yet, through allowing that feeling, you can learn how to observe and examine your internal dialogue—*your thoughts and your self-talk.* After all, that is where pressure is really created, and when you get to know it, let it go. Many examples have been given. You know what to do. Now you just have to go out and do it. Soon you will be able to say goodbye to pressure. Good luck!

TEN POINTS ON WINNING WITH THE FOCUS EDGE APPROACH

1. PRESSURE DEPENDS ON YOU

Why is it that some athletes respond to pressure with stress while others take joy in the challenge? Some super-athletes actually look forward to pressure. Jack Nicklaus: "Pressure situations are what I strive to get involved in.... Pressure is the fun of the game." Performance anxiety is not always the result of a pressure situation—at least not for all. Where do you fit in to this puzzle?

2. YOU CAN CONTROL PERFORMANCE ANXIETY

Performance anxiety requires believing that (1) you might fail in front of important people (2) who can judge you and (3) that you focus on your own fear of failure. You can prevent this anxiety by (1) making the people less important (at least in your mind) by focusing on your confidence rather than your insecurity, (2) accepting that you might fail and that would be OK, or (3) merely by switching the focus off yourself. Any of these choices will prevent, or at least significantly decrease, any performance anxiety.

3. ONE WAY OF DEALING WITH PRESSURE IS TO KNOW YOUR LIMITS

If you come prepared to do your best and are able to perform to the best of your ability, then there is nothing more you can ask of yourself. Wade Boggs took hundreds of ground balls before a game to prepare psychologically. Jack Nicklaus gave every game his best, and "if I lose after having given it my best effort, so be it." Knowing your limits and playing within those limits also lessens the pressure. Deion Sanders: "I know my limits. But within those limits, I have no limits." Know your limits. Play the best within those limits and the pressure begins to evaporate.

4. ANOTHER WAY IS TO JUST GIVE YOUR EGO A REST

If you can keep your ego out of the picture, then performance anxiety decreases. If your body feels tense, let it be—don't let it affect your mind or self-confidence. Be present in the moment and lose yourself in the game instead of thinking about how you're performing. See yourself more as a performer making people happy rather than as a competitor. Realize that even if you mess up, your family will still love and accept you. Even if you don't meet expectations, at least you're in the game, not in the bleachers like everyone else. In other words, relax—it's just a game.

5. THE BEST ANTIDOTE TO PRESSURE IS GOOD PREPARATION

Sports would be nothing without pressure. The greater the pressure, the more enjoyable the game. It's all about how athletes deal with the pressure. Some do it well; some don't. American astronauts were chosen on the basis of "having the right stuff." That meant they wouldn't panic in a crisis and could be counted on to do what was necessary, even when Houston was notified that there was a problem. As an athlete, the simplest thing you can do to diminish performance anxiety is to be as prepared as you can. "In judo," said Doug Rogers, "the competition is the easy part. How you get there is what's difficult."

6. THE NEXT BEST ANTIDOTE IS TO FOCUS ON PERFORMANCE GOALS RATHER THAN RESULT GOALS

Ultimately, you have no control over how things turn out. As a batter, you can't control the pitch or whether your hit will be caught, but you do have some control over how you hit the ball. You have no control over the results but all the control over your performance. If you select performance goals, you maintain control, and this will lessen your pressure and anxiety. "I came to Chicago with no expectations. None." said Michael Jordan. "The only pressure I felt when I went to the NBA was to prove I deserved to play on that level."

7. PRACTICE THE KEY ELEMENTS OF YOUR PERFORMANCE

In order to have better control over your performance, be sure to isolate the key movements or skills or knowledge you need in order to ensure your success, and practice, practice, practice. It may be swinging through the strike zone, throwing the football while being rushed, running the final lap at a certain speed, or your backhand in tennis. Whatever it is, identify it and conquer it. Once you conquer that most challenging aspect of your game, nothing else will make you as anxious.

8. GET RID OF PRESSURE THE "SPOILER" WAY

If you're in a situation where you're the underdog and the opposition has a record of beating you, then you may feel under pressure. If you take the stand that, regardless of win or lose, you're going to have fun by playing all out, then you've already won in a sense. If you lose, it was expected, but if you win by playing all out for the fun of it, then what an upset! This relieves the pressure for your team because you do have control over how much effort you put into the game, so you go in with a sense of control and much less to lose than the opposition.

9. FOCUS ON WHAT YOU DO, NOT WHAT THE OPPOSITION DOES

As long as you perform to the best of your ability, what the opposition does is not your responsibility. Be aware of it, but do not make it your responsibility. Mark Davis learned to pitch accurately according to his catcher's signals and not pay heed to the batter. As a surgeon slicing up the strike zone, he focused on what he could do so well and was less distracted by the presence of the various batters he faced. As a result, Mark went on to win the Cy Young award while setting the save record for the San Diego Padres.

10. WHEN INTIMIDATED BY THE CROWD, LEARN TO "SUCK" ENERGY FROM IT, WHETHER THEY CHEER OR BOO

Nothing like an antagonistic crowd to lead to performance anxiety, but if you learn to use that negative energy, then it works in your favor. Boxer Tommy Morrison was taught to suck energy from the crowd, as if through a straw, to energize him, and he ended up defeating the formidable George Foreman for the heavyweight championship. Learn to use the energy that's available to build your strength. Transform the performance anxiety into useful energy.

CONCLUSION

THE FOCUS EDGE MINDSET

You have now had a chance to see how super-athletes approach competition in their sports. You have been able to get "inside" their heads and learn how they deal with the "Big Three"—*motivation, confidence*, and *concentration*. In addition, you have read how they deal with the "Big Three" when they are in *pressure situations*. We will now summarize the main elements of the Focus Edge mindset for you.

It is our belief that this mindset is what sets the super-athlete apart from less successful competitors. By using as many of these nine suggestions as possible, you will have a greater chance of achieving your goals—both athletic and non-athletic alike.

1. **Have a strong desire to succeed coupled sometimes with a strong desire to avoid failure.**

The simplest way to follow this suggestion successfully is to become involved in something that you love, something that you have a passion for. It suggests that you not spend extra time on things that don't matter that much to you. Identify what is important to you, what really matters to you. It was clear from our interviews that super-athletes truly love what they do. This produces an intensity in them that is quite remarkable. Their desire to win or avoid failure can move them to great lengths. As Michael Jordan said, "If it is just a game, then it is the game that I want to win." When you are engaged in something with this type of significance, something that is important to you, the desire to be successful comes naturally.

Although fear can sometimes be a part of this desire, it is always best to focus on the desirable rather than the fearful aspect of this goal in pressure situations. "Encouraged by tournament results and various teachers," judoka expert Doug Rogers told us, "I realized that maybe, just maybe, I could become a champion." Remember that there is nothing "wrong" with wanting to avoid failure. Super-athletes want to avoid it as much as anyone else. Chris Evert said, "... because I hate to lose, not because of the thrill of victory." This type of intensity leads people to put everything they have into avoiding failure. However, it is not the object of their concentration. Rather, they focus on what needs to be done in order to be successful.

2. Take on challenges.

Super-athletes relish challenges. The challenges they accept are what give "spice" to their performances. Can you recall the types of challenges that the greatest athletes accepted? They were *mastery, achievement,* and *competence.* Ted Williams wanted to master the art of hitting a baseball. Michael Jordan wanted to achieve one more championship. Craig Biggio wants to be able to do lots of things well on the baseball field and show his competence. You can turn anything into a challenge by attempting to master it, by accomplishing more in that specific area, or by simply proving to yourself that you can do it well or even better than you used to do it. Even something as simple as ironing a load of clothes can be framed as a challenge—the challenge can be to iron each piece perfectly (mastery) or to get the entire load done in a certain amount of time (achievement). Pick the particular type of challenge that appeals most to you. Remember Deion Sanders' observation: play within your limits, but within those limits set no limits. Create a challenge and then go for it.

3. Select controllable goals.

Super-athletes know themselves and their abilities. They choose smaller, performance goals that they are confident they can meet. Ted Williams, for example, chose the very simple goal of making an optimal swing through the strike zone. This was something he felt he could control. Hal McCrae had a goal of hitting the ball hard. This was not totally under his control, but he believed he could do it. This confidence can come from past performances, including something as simple as a practice session. Remember, when Gordie Howe was in a scoring slump, he drew confidence from scoring a goal in practice! So set goals that you know you have the ability to meet. It may take the setting of several smaller goals, each of which you know you can do, in order for you to reach your final goal. Don't be deterred. If you set small performance goals you know you can reach, your confidence will be high and so will your motivation.

4. Know what you can do

In order to set controllable goals that will help you reach your final goals, it is important to *know yourself.* It is important to know both your strengths and weaknesses. It takes a strong person to know his/her limitations, to admit those to oneself. Sit down and do an analysis of your abilities and liabilities. Deion Sanders realized that he was never going to be a home run hitter. This was one of his limitations. So, he focused on his strengths—his speed and his incredible athletic ability. Within these limits he would set goals for himself. Mark Price knew he was not the biggest, strongest, or quickest guard in the NBA, so, he built his game on making his teammates better and being an accurate shooter when he did decide to shoot. You might even ask people that know you well to give you some input. Remember that we are talking about you really knowing, having a sense of certainty, that you can do something. Once you know what you can do, you will be able to set more realistic goals.

5. Focus on past successes.

Motivation is much more than just wanting something very badly. Many people want something badly, but still don't have the necessary motivation to go after it. An important part of motivation is confidence. If people do not believe that they know how to do something or do not believe they have the ability to do it, their motivation will be weakened. So, look at your past successes and get first-hand evidence that you have the ability to reach your goal. Remember, Michael Jordan said he only needed to do something one time to really know he could do it. Super-athletes sometimes even use success in practice to remind themselves that they can do something. The legendary Gordie Howe would use a goal scored in practice to build his confidence when he was in a scoring slump. You can *choose your performance history*! It is sometimes helpful to have other people point out some of our accomplishments—our culture makes "bragging" or "blowing one's own horn" a no-no. As a result, we can forget some of our own accomplishments. What is important is that you know you have the ability and the know-how to accomplish your goals. This will keep motivation at its highest.

6. Prepare thoroughly.

Super-athletes invariably are the best-prepared competitors on the field. Johnny Unitas would spend hours studying films of upcoming opponents until he knew their tendencies and weaknesses like the back of his hand. Ted Williams not only studied opposing pitchers but umpires as well; he wanted to know what a particular pitcher would most likely throw and what a particular umpire would most likely call. Their preparation serves two purposes: (1) it boosts their confidence, because they know that they have done what is needed to be prepared; and (2) their preparation gives them something to think about and focus on prior to the competition. This helps keep distracting thoughts from entering their minds, leading to anxiety and pressure. On game day have a well-established routine or ritual you can perform leading up to the competition. It will help keep your mind focused in a positive fashion.

7. Make performance goals important.

Although you will have your main goal in the back of your mind, it is critical that you make your performance goals important. These are the things you need to do in order to be successful. You need to make carrying out your performance goals the most important thing to you. Carrying out your performance goals must become more important than things like pleasing the crowd, worrying about what might happen if you fail, or just about anything else. The more important you can make your performance goals, the more likely you are to accomplish them. When performance goals are met, the likelihood of achieving your major goals is very high. If, for example, you want to write a book, a performance goal might be sitting and writing twice a day for an hour at a time. To increase your chances of success, you must make sitting and writing more important than just about anything else you could spend your time doing. If you want to be the best third baseman in the league, you might set a performance goal of fielding 100 ground balls a day. You need to make that goal more important than any other goal at the time. Don't let anything come in front of that activity. It is what the super-athletes do. It works.

8. Open up or narrow the field of attention as the situation demands.

Different situations demand different widths in your field of attention. As a quarterback, you need a wider field of attention as you look over the defense. Batting in baseball, you need a very narrow field of attention as the pitcher starts to release the ball. If you have to repair a leaking faucet and have little time to finish it, you need a narrow field of attention—forget the TV, forget washing the car, forget it all—except the wrench and the gasket in front of you. If you have to drive through heavy traffic, you need to look around and broaden your attention.

9. Focus only on what is happening from moment-to-moment.

Keep your thoughts and your attention in the present moment. If you are a batter getting ready to step into the batter's box, you need to have your thoughts focused on what you are doing—what is your goal? It might be to hit a good pitch or to make an optimal swing or to hit the ball hard. When you get in the box your focus needs to narrow down to the ball, picking it up when it leaves the pitcher's hand. There is no time to be thinking about other things—problems at home, what might happen if you don't get a hit, etc. Nancy Lopez felt as if she was "alone" on the golf course. Her concentration was directed only towards what she was doing. Racecar drivers like Mario Andretti and Richard Petty stress the necessity of focusing only on what is happening at the moment. Their sport demands it.

Here is a summary of the "Big Three" for you: motivation, confidence, and concentration. These are the three factors that super-athletes pointed to, almost unanimously, when asked why they were so successful.

MOTIVATION

Motivation is a willingness to make the effort to fulfill a goal. Included here is the desire to achieve a goal as well as a belief that one knows how to achieve the goal and has the necessary abilities. Super-athletes possess both the intense desire to achieve their goals and the confidence that they can do it. Often *fear* is mixed with *desire* in these goals, but self-confidence is never lost. This results in an *intensity* that is missing in most other athletes. Such intensity can be expressed in aggressive play. However, it is just as likely to be observed in quiet, steely concentration.

CONFIDENCE

Confidence is feeling in control. It comes from two areas: *past successes* and *performance goals*. Super-athletes have a ready performance history to draw upon. In some cases just one or two occurrences may be enough to give the necessary confidence. Performance goals, because they are under an athlete's control, also lead to confidence. Because super-athletes are confident, they have fewer distracting thoughts about potential failure. The "what if I fail" thoughts that plague so many of us are much less of a problem for the super-athlete.

CONCENTRATION

Concentration is being aware with focused attention that is sustained for a given period of time. This attention is directed both outward on the activities the athlete needs to perform and inward on the moment-to-moment flow of the athlete's experience. Outward attention may be directed on objects such as the rim (when shooting free throws), an opponent's hands when boxing, on an offensive lineman's stance when playing defense in football, or a competitor's car when racing. Inward attention may be directed toward strategic thoughts such as when to pass an opposing runner, what type of pitch to expect from a certain pitcher, or when to come to the net behind an approach shot in tennis. It may even be something as simple as reminding oneself to take a deep breath. The important idea there is that super-athletes are "in the moment" at the point of action. They are aware and present, to *focus on what they are doing*—the steps they are taking to meet their goals. Major goals (like winning) as well as strategic plans (how to go about winning) are in the background of the super-athlete's attention. Focus is sustained through *preparation*, including game plans, visualizations, rituals, and the like. This prepared thinking and imaging keeps the mind busy and prevents negative thoughts from emerging. Super-athletes are able to do this because they make preparation more important than anything else at the time.

There you have it. Now you know what super-athletes know. You know what you can do to improve your performance. Knowing what you know is, of course, no guarantee that you will become a super-athlete. However, using the Focus Edge mindset will help you reach goals that are realistically within your reach.

A super-athlete would not wait to start meeting important goals. Neither should you.

- Accept the challenge of sitting down, right now, and making a plan.
- Select a main goal. Make sure it is something that you love or is of major importance to you.
- Identify your strengths and weaknesses.
- Select performance goals that will help you reach your main goal.
- Are you certain that you have the ability to achieve these performance goals? If not, go back a step and select a performance goal that you are certain you can meet.
- Set aside a time for yourself to work solely on meeting that goal. During that time make meeting that performance goal the single most important thing you can do.
- Practice being concentrated and aware in the moment.
- Every time you meet a performance goal, no matter how small, point it out to yourself. Say it out loud. "I did it. I met my goal." This will boost your confidence for your next performance goal.

Now you have the secrets of the legends that made sports history. Use the information you've learned wisely. You're on your path to success!

Biographical Sketches

The following are biographical sketches of super-athletes from different sports selected from our research.

AUTO RACING

Mario Andretti

In 1965, Mario joined a professional racing team and won the United States Auto Club national championship. The first time he competed in the Indianapolis 500, he placed third and was named Rookie of the Year. In 1969, Mario won the Indianapolis 500.

At only 5 feet 6 inches tall, Mario was considered by many to be too small for racing, but this was overridden by his powerful wrists, hands, and shoulders, his mechanical expertise, and his extraordinary stamina and determination. Moreover, Mario had a reputation for staying cool under pressure.

In 1978, Mario won the international racing world's most coveted prize, the Formula One world championship. Known for its treacherous winding roads, Formula One racing was entirely different from racing on the oval track. Mario became known for his versatility, winning on more than 100 different types of tracks and courses. He was the first driver in motor racing history to win both the Indianapolis and Formula One titles. In 1984, he won Driver of the Year, becoming the only individual to have won this award in each of three consecutive decades. Mario Andretti became the premier auto racer in America, and later in the world.

Don Garlits

Champion drag racer Don Garlits is a man of many accomplishments. Aside from his extraordinary successes on the drag strip, he is the founder of the Garlits' Classic Car and International Drag Racing Hall of Fame. Currently, he writes an automotive advice column for Tribune Media Services.

Garlits began racing in 1950. He won his first major race in 1955 and has been rewriting the record books ever since. Garlits, whose nickname "Big Daddy" is a registered trademark, is considered an unequaled authority on the subject of automobile mechanics. His technical expertise is responsible for many innovations in drag racing, including the use of motorcycle-style wheels and the design of today's rear-engine streamlined Top Fuel Dragsters. Garlits built and raced 34 custom dragsters in the famous record-shattering "Swamp Rat" series.

With a personal top speed of 287.81 miles per hour (mph), "Big Daddy" has made over 5,000 runs down the quarter mile over 200 mph. He held the NHRA Official World Record at 207.8 mph and the AHRA Official World Record of 260.49 mph. Along the way, "Big Daddy" picked up more than 6 million dollars in race earnings. After more than 30 years as a champion competing on racetracks all over the country, including the flight deck of the aircraft carrier USS *Lexington*, winning over 140 national events, Don Garlits has established himself as a name synonymous with drag racing.

Richard Petty

Richard Petty was one of the greatest drivers ever. He competed in 513 consecutive Winston Cup races, a NASCAR record, and led everyone in Winston Cup victories and super speedway wins. Richard became sport's first million-dollar driver after the Dixie 500 in August 1971 in Atlanta, Georgia. He surpassed 7 million dollars in earnings at the Daytona 500 in 1990.

Petty made his racing debut on July 18, 1958, in Toronto, Canada. His first win came in a 100-mile convertible race on the old Columbia (SC) dirt track in 1959, while his first Winston Cup win came at Charlotte (NC) in 1960. His first super speedway win was in the Daytona 500 on February 14, 1964. Among his many awards were winning seven WCS championships, Winston Cup Series Rookie of the Year in 1959, Driver of the Year in 1971, 9 years voted Most Popular Winston Cup Driver, inducted into the North Carolina Athletic Hall of Fame, named American Auto Racing Writers and Broadcasters Association's most outstanding driver, and selected by AARWBA as Man of the Year in 1992 for contributions on and off the track.

Petty's major victories included seven wins at the Daytona 500, seven at the Rockingham Carolina 500, five at the Dover Budweiser 500, and big wins at Atlanta, Pocono, Talladega, and Darlington. The Richard Petty/STP sponsorship which began with a victory at the Winston Western 500 at Riverside (CA) International Raceway on January 23, 1972, is the longest sponsor/driver relationship in motor sports history. Overall, Richard Petty will be remembered as one of auto racing's most outstanding athletes.

BASEBALL

Hank Aaron

In his first year with the Milwaukee Braves minor league system, Hank batted .336, hit nine home runs, had 61 runs batted in (RBIs), was chosen for the All-Star team, and was named the league's Rookie of the Year. After continued success in the minors, Hank was moved up to the major leagues in 1954. He was to play left field for the Braves.

In 1957, Milwaukee won the World Series. Hank batted .322, led the league with 44 home runs, and had 132 RBIs. In addition, he was named the National League's Most Valuable Player. Although a gifted hitter, Hank worked hard on his base-running skills. In 1963, he became only the fifth player in history to steal more than 30 bases and hit more than 30 home runs.

The Braves moved to Atlanta in 1966. Hank kept hitting home runs and approaching Babe Ruth's record. On April 4, 1974, he hit home run number 714, tying Ruth. A few days later, he broke the record with a powerful home run against the Los Angeles Dodgers. He had become the greatest home run hitter of all time. By the time he retired in 1976, Hank had achieved several batting records that included most runs batted in, most extra-base hits, and most total bases, and the record for most career home runs.

Jeff Bagwell

Jeff had a career .413 batting average at the University of Hartford and was inducted into the university's Athletic Hall of Fame. Following college, he signed with the Red Sox and then the Houston Astros. His minor league highlights included hitting .366 in the Florida Instructional League, being named Most Valuable Player in the Eastern League in 1990 after hitting .333 for New Britain, and being named to the TOPPS Double A All-Star team.

Upon arriving in the major leagues, Jeff became the first Houston Astro player ever to win the BBWAA's National League Rookie of the Year award in 1991. He led the Astros in home runs, RBIs, walks, slugging, and on-base percentage. Jeff was named *Baseball America's* Major League Rookie of the Year, the top rookie position player on the *Sporting News* postseason All-Star team and was a part of the TOPPS Major League Rookie All-Star team. He finished among the top hitters in the National League, hitting .320 in 1993 despite missing the final 20 games of the season because of a broken bone in his left hand. The injury ended his streak of consecutive games played at 304, the longest in club history. In 1994, Jeff was a unanimous selection by the Baseball Writers of America as National League MVP. During this year, he set numerous club records while batting .368, setting a home run mark by hitting his 38th in just 106 games, and earning the Rawlings Gold Glove Award as well as the *Sporting News* award for best offensive player at his position. He became the first player since Carl Yazstremski to finish first or second in the league in average, runs, RBIs, and homers. In 1995, Jeff was the first player in club history to lead the team in RBIs for five consecutive seasons and in 1996 established club single-season records for doubles, extra-base hits, total bases, and RBIs, while being named for the second time to the NL All-Star team.

Jeff Bagwell is a super-athlete. He excels both offensively and defensively at his position. He has been a consistent .300 hitter with exceptional fielding percentages. As an all-around team player, Jeff Bagwell has been a key to the success of the Houston Astros.

CRAIG BIGGIO

Craig Biggio was one of the finest all-around players in the game. He could beat you with the bat, the glove, or on the base paths. He was voted on the National League All-Star team on numerous occasions and led the Houston Astros to a number of division titles. Although Craig Biggio was a catcher, he was rock solid at second base, and his versatility as a ballplayer was second to none.

Craig's baseball career took off while at Seton Hall University. While at Seton Hall, he was named first team All-America and batted .407 with 14 homers and 68 RBIs in 1987. He joined the class-A Asheville team after signing with the Houston Astros that same year. His development was so rapid that he was able to make the jump to the major leagues with less than 500 minor league at-bats in 1988. His first full season in the major leagues saw him establish himself as one of the top offensive players in the game.

In 1990, Craig became the first Astros catcher ever to lead the team in batting and be named to the All-Star team. In the '90s, he consistently was ranked among the league leaders in at-bats, hits, doubles, total bases, runs, walks, extra base hits, stolen bases, hit by pitch, and hardest to strike out. Moreover, he was a regular team leader in homers and batting average for the Astros. He earned the *Sporting News* Silver Slugger Award as the best offensive player at his position as well as the Rawlings Gold Glove Award as the league's top defensive second baseman. Craig Biggio could do a many things. He was a super team player as well as a superstar at his position.

WADE BOGGS

In high school, Wade was an outstanding athlete in football as well as baseball. He signed a contract to play baseball in the Boston Red Sox organization in 1978. Wade was promoted to the major leagues after leading the league at Pawtucket with a .335 batting average. He made an immediate impact on the Boston Red Sox, hitting .349. In the years to follow Wade continued to terrorize American League pitchers, winning four straight batting championships from 1985 to 1988 with averages of .368, .357, .363, and .366. He led his team to an American League Championship Series in 1986. Wade's regular season performances resulted in being the starting third baseman for the American League All-Star teams from 1985 through 1991.

Wade Boggs became one of the premier hitters and third basemen by constant practice and determination. He overcame many problems on and off the field to restore his image. His lifetime batting average is one of the highest ever. In 1999, he hit a home run and became a member of the elite 3000 hit club while with the Tampa Bay Devil Rays. With these accomplishments, Wade has written his name in the record books as one of the greatest hitters ever.

MARK DAVIS

Davis began his career with the Philadelphia Phillies in 1980 and then spent parts of five seasons with the San Francisco Giants. He established himself as a top reliever during the 1987 season with the San Diego Padres. In 1988, he became the Padres' closer, appearing in the All-Star games. He won the Cy Young Award in 1989, becoming the fourth closer so honored till 2003, when Eric Gagne took over that distinction. His career continued with stints with the Kansas City Royals, the Atlanta Braves, and the Milwaukee Brewers.

Cecil Fielder

Cecil was in the minor leagues from 1982 till 1985. In this time, he was twice named to the All-Star team and was consistently among the league leaders in home runs and RBIs. In 1985, he was promoted from AA Knoxville to Toronto. He began his major league career with a five-game hitting streak and played with the Blue Jays through 1988.

Cecil joined the Detroit Tigers in 1990. Being a prolific home run hitter, he hit 51 in 1990, which made him only the 11th player in major league history to hit 50. From 1990 to 1996, Cecil has led the majors and his club in home runs, RBIs, total bases, slugging percentage, and extra base hits on numerous occasions. He led the majors in RBIs for three consecutive years and became only the second player in AL history to do so. Cecil was selected as the *Sporting News* AL Player of the Year in 1990 and was placed on the 1990, '91, '92, and '93 All-Star teams. In 1996, he was traded to the Yankees and promptly helped them win the American League pennant and World Series. In the postseason, he hit .308 and was named Babe Ruth Award winner as World Series MVP by the New York Chapter of the BBWAA.

In 1997, Cecil Fielder was the major league leader for home runs and RBIs. He was ahead of such baseball greats as Barry Bonds, Ken Griffey, and Frank Thomas. Cecil was one of the most dangerous hitters in the game with men on base. He has proven himself to be one of the great long ball hitters of all time.

Ken Griffey, Sr.

The Cincinnati Reds selected Ken in the 1969 draft. From 1969 to 1973, he was a consistent .300 plus hitter in the minors. He made his major league debut in late 1973, impressing the club by batting .384 in 25 games. He then became a mainstay for the Reds for 19 major league seasons. He was particularly brilliant in helping to guide what had become known as the Big Red Machine to consecutive World Series

Championships while batting .305 and .336 (second in the NL), respectively, in those two seasons. Ken was selected on All-Star teams and won a number of MVP awards while batting over .300 numerous times for the Reds.

Over his lengthy career, Ken was traded to the New York Yankees, the Atlanta Braves, and finally the Seattle Mariners. Hitting a remarkable .611, he was the league's premier pinch hitter in 1987. Ken Griffey finished his career with a .296 batting average and at least one home run against every club in major league baseball except Cleveland. Following his retirement as an active player, Ken Griffey used his skills as a coach in the major leagues.

TONY GWYNN

At San Diego State, Tony became a legend. He excelled in both basketball and baseball. He established a record for assists in basketball and hit .301, .423, and .416 in three seasons of baseball. After his final baseball season, the San Diego Padres drafted him. Through exceptional performances, Tony quickly moved through the Padres minor league system. In 1982, he began his career in the major leagues.

In his first complete season, Tony won the National League batting title in 1984 with a .351 average. He also led all of baseball in hits and multiple hit games while leading the Padres to the World Series. In the years to come, he was consistently chosen on the National League All-Star team and won four Gold Glove awards for his defensive play. In 1987, he set a club record by hitting .370 and in 1989, he won his fourth National League batting championship. Finally, in 1990, Tony reached another milestone in his career with 1,500 hits.

Tony Gwynn has often been referred to as the "ultimate hitting machine." He is well known for having exceptional bat control and as a hitter who can hit off-speed pitches, rarely striking out. With a lifetime batting average of .328 that is coupled with all his other accomplishments, Tony Gwynn has earned all the respect given to him and must be considered as one of the greatest contact hitters in the history of baseball.

SANDY KOUFAX

Sanford "Sandy" Koufax is a member of Baseball's Hall of Fame, becoming the youngest player ever elected in 1972. He was one of the most dominant pitchers to ever play the game. During the five seasons from 1962 to 1966 he led the major leagues in ERA for five consecutive years, a record that still stands. He won three Cy Young Awards—in 1963, 1965, and 1966. In 1963 he also won the NL MVP award—the last pitcher in the National League to do so. During that five-year period he pitched 100 complete games, 33 of them shutouts. During this same period he pitched four no-hitters—one of which was a perfect game. Baseball has never seen such pitching dominance.

Koufax struggled early in his career, especially with his control. Once he learned to throw his blazing fastball and biting curve for strikes, he became almost unhittable. He was so dominant that he led the league in strikeouts four times, struck out 382 batters in the 1965 season (a record that still stands), and twice fanned 18 hitters in a game. Sandy was forced to retire after the 1966 season due to traumatic arthritis in his throwing arm. When he finally stopped pitching, he had numbers that may never be matched.

BARRY LARKIN

At the University of Michigan, Barry was the first baseball player ever to be named Most Valuable Player of the Big Ten twice. He earned All America honors and hit .311 for the U.S. Olympic team in 1984. In the minor leagues, he was on the TOPPS AAA All-Star team and was selected American Association MVP and Rookie-of-the-Year with Denver. Barry was promoted to the Reds in 1986.

In his early years with the Reds, Barry was the ball club's most consistent hitter. He closed the 1988 season with a 21-game hitting streak, led all major league hitters for fewest strikeouts, and earned five straight Silver Slugger awards. Later, Barry was consistently among the league leaders in batting average, RBIs, home runs, and stolen bases. He became the first shortstop to hit .300 or better over five consecutive seasons in 40 years. In 1995, he successfully stole 51 bases in 56 attempts. He was only the fourth player in major league history to compile such a success ratio. Defensively, he has earned several Rawlings Gold Glove awards. In 1996, Barry became the first shortstop in major league history to join the elite "30-30 Club" (30 home runs and 30 stolen bases).

For his many achievements, he was selected as the Reds MVP in 1990 and 1991 and National League MVP by the Baseball Writers Association of America in 1995. And, adding to this, Barry was named eight times to the National League All-Star team. Barry Larkin is unique. He was a great all-around ball player who could win games in many different ways.

WILLIE MAYS

Willie signed a contract with the New York Giants on the day he graduated from high school in 1950. After a brief but successful stay in the minor leagues, he was brought up to the majors in 1951. Under popular manager Leo Durocher, the Giants won the National League pennant in 1951. Willie was credited as being the "spark" that won the victory.

In leading the Giants to a 1954 World Series victory over the Cleveland Indians, Willie made a catch that has been widely acclaimed as the greatest ever made on a baseball field. He was an exceptional defensive player because of his famous catches and strong throws from the outfield. Aside from his defensive skills, Willie was a great hitter. With a .345 batting average and 41 home runs, he led the league in 1954. Over the years numerous awards have been showered on him. When the Giants moved to San Francisco, Willie continued his great performances. In 1965, he hit 52 home runs and was named the National League's Most Valuable Player.

In 1979, Willie was inducted into the Baseball Hall of Fame. With 660 home runs, he ranks as one of the all-time home-run hitters along with Hank Aaron and Babe Ruth. Considering all his record-breaking achievements, Willie Mays has earned a place among those super-athletes who have performed at the highest levels of their sport. And as an entertainer at his position, he was one-of-a-kind.

HAL McRAE

Hal played 23 years of pro baseball with four years in the minors and 19 in the majors. He was drafted by the Cincinnati Reds in 1965 and made his major league debut in 1968. Hal spent his entire career with the Reds and the Kansas City Royals. He helped lead the '70 and '72 Reds to titles. Hal played with the Royals from 1973 to 1987. During this time, he hit over .300 six times, including a career high .332 in 1976. In addition, he led the majors and set a club record with 133 RBIs in 1982. Hal was a three time All-Star and three-time Designated Hitter of the Year. He was the Royals' Player of the Year twice. Playing in eight League Championship Series and four World Series, Hal set an LCS record for most runs in a five-game series, tied a record for career doubles, and hit .400 in 17 World Series games.

Hal McRae was an outstanding hitter. He was a student of the game. Hal followed his playing career with managing and coaching positions and was elected to the American League All-Star Game coaching staff in 1992.

Overall, Hal McRae was a super-athlete and continues to impart his abundant knowledge of the game to younger players.

STAN MUSIAL

Stan "The Man" Musial is a baseball legend. Beginning in high school, Stan was an exceptional athlete. He turned down a basketball scholarship to sign a professional baseball contract with the St. Louis Cardinals. His major league career, all with the Cardinals, stretched from 1941 to 1963. He was the first player in the National League to reach the $100,000-per-year salary figure.

Stan's athletic awards, records, and recognitions are extensive. He was Most Valuable Player in the National League (1943,1946, and 1948) and a member of the National League All-Star Team (1943, 1944, and 1946 through 1963). He was selected as MVP by the Baseball Writers (1946), League Player of the Year by the *Sporting News* (1946 and 1951), Sid Mercer Award winner by the New York Baseball Writers (1947), Kennesaw Mountain Landis Memorial Plaque winner (1948), and *Sports Illustrated* Sportsman of the Year (1957). He also won the Freedom Leadership Medal in 1968.

Stan "The Man" is truly one of baseball's greatest hitters. He won seven Batting Titles—1943, '46, '48, '50, '51, '52, and '57. He was fully recognized for his many achievements in 1969. At that time, Stan Musial was inducted into the Baseball Hall of Fame.

BABE RUTH

Early in his career, Babe was a starting pitcher for the Boston Red Sox from 1915 through 1918. During that time, he won 78 games and lost only 40 as the Red Sox won three championships. Babe was also one of Boston's best hitters and was used as an outfielder so that he could play every day. Babe led the league in homers in 1919. At the end of the season, he was sold to the New York Yankees in what turned out to be the worst deal in the history of baseball for the Red Sox.

Babe flourished in New York, leading the Yankees to seven World Series victories and four championships. In 1920, Babe hit 54 home runs. In 1921, he hit 59 homers while batting .378. Ruth became known as "The Sultan of Swat." Long home runs were called "Ruthian" shots and the new Yankee Stadium was nicknamed "The House That Ruth Built." In 1927, Ruth did the unthinkable. He set the all-time record for home runs in a single season by hitting 60 of them. What distinguished Babe from other great home run hitters was his ability to hit homers under extreme pressure.

Babe was elected to the National Baseball Hall of Fame in 1936. He had hit 714 career home runs, leading the American League twelve times in single-season totals. He had a lifetime batting average of .342 and set the all-time slugging average of .690. Babe became a legend. This extraordinary athlete, one of the twentieth century's greatest, came to symbolize America's national pastime.

ALAN TRAMMELL

Alan was an outstanding baseball and basketball star. He entered the minor leagues playing for Bristol and Montgomery in 1976 and 1977. Alan was voted Southern League 1977 Most Valuable Player. He moved up to the Detroit Tigers in 1978 where he was named to *Baseball Bulletin's* 1978 Rookie All-Star Team.

From 1980 to 1989, Alan was voted Tiger of the Year three times, led the team in stolen bases for two years, won four Gold Gloves, and was selected for five American League All-Star teams. In 1987, he became the first Tiger with 200 hits and 100 RBIs since Al Kaline in 1955. Alan won the World Series MVP Award with the highest average (.450), most hits (9), and total bases (16) as a member of one of the greatest Tiger teams ever.

After a variety of injuries through 1992, he made a remarkable comeback in 1993 following a fractured right ankle suffered in Kansas City. Alan batted over .300 (.329) for the seventh time in his career. With second baseman Lou Whitaker, he established an AL record of 1,918 appearances together. Moreover, he tied Hall of Famer Charlie Gehringer for twelfth on Tigers' all-time home run list with 184. Overall, Alan is among the all-time leaders in most offensive categories and established himself as one of baseball's greatest shortstops.

MATT WILLIAMS

The San Francisco Giants drafted Matt out of the University of Nevada at Las Vegas in 1986. He had a brief stay in the minor leagues in 1986, 1987, and parts of 1988 and 1989. His 44 homers in 1989 ranked second in professional baseball. His nine RBIs set an NLCS record for five games. Matt played through 1996 with the San Francisco Giants before being traded to Cleveland in 1997. While in San Francisco, he became with Barry Bonds one of the most lethal and feared one-two punches in baseball.

Over his career, Matt Williams had 20 or more home runs in each of his seven full seasons in the majors. He was a consistent member of the National League All-Star team and has numerous Rawlings Gold Glove awards and Silver Slugger awards. He is ranked fourth in Giant history for career home runs and tenth in RBIs. Most notable were his 43 homers in the strike-shortened season of 1994. That total led the majors and put him on a pace to equal the then all-time home run mark of 61 set by Roger Maris and broke the NL mark of 56.

Matt Williams was a complete ball player. He could field and he could hit. Matt played the game with great intensity and was an unquestionable super-athlete at his position.

TED WILLIAMS

In 1938 with Minneapolis, Ted led the league in batting average (.366), home runs (42), and RBIs (142). He was promoted to the Boston Red Sox in 1939. During his first season, Ted batted .327, hit 31 home runs, and drove in a league-leading 145 runs. Ted was a tough competitor and a perfectionist. After batting .344 the following season, he was determined to improve on that. Improve on that he did. In 1941, he ended the season batting .406. This was an amazing accomplishment. To date, no one else had been able to finish an entire season with a batting average of .400 or better.

Ted won the Most Valuable Player award and helped the Red Sox make it to the World Series in 1946. After that, he won his second Triple Crown in 1947 and second MVP award in 1949. Ted returned from the Marine reserves and won batting titles in 1957 and 1958, when he was 38 and 39 years old. For his career, he ranks among the highest in slugging average (.634) and batting average (.344). Ted Williams was voted into the National Baseball Hall of Fame in 1966. Many baseball experts would agree that this left-handed hitter was the greatest of all-time.

Ted passed away on July 5, 2002.

BASKETBALL

CHARLES BARKLEY

"Sir Charles" was one of the most prolific and colorful athletes to ever play in the NBA. Many questioned the Philadelphia 76ers for selecting him out of Auburn University as the fifth pick overall in the 1984 draft. "Experts" wondered if the seemingly overweight "round mound of rebound" would be able to make it in the NBA. Undersized for a front line player (barely over 6 feet 4 inches), Barkley quickly proved the 76ers knew what they were doing. He was named to the all-rookie team in 1984 and then went on to become an NBA All-Star for 10 straight seasons. He was selected to the first two Dream Teams for the 1992 and 1996 Olympics. He is one of a few players in league history to score 20,000 points, grab 12,000 rebounds, and hand out 4,000 assists.

Barkley used his immense strength and a great sense of timing to become one of the best all-around players in the game. He was too strong for smaller players to guard and too quick for bigger players. He worked at his game and toward the end of his career became an excellent shooter to go along with his always-wonderful rebounding skills. At the end of his career, even opposing fans grew to love "Sir Charles."

LARRY BIRD

At Indiana State, Larry turned a mediocre team into a contender for the National Collegiate Athletic Association (NCAA) championship. National attention was suddenly drawn to this exceptional player. Then in 1979, as a senior, Larry led his team to the championship game of the NCAA Tournament against Michigan State and Magic Johnson. Larry and Magic were to become the two dominant players of the next decade.

The Boston Celtics of the National Basketball Association (NBA) chose Larry in the first round of the 1978 NBA draft. In his first season, he was selected as NBA Rookie of the Year as he led the Celtics to an excellent record. In 1980, the Celtics won the NBA Championship. In 1984, Larry was named NBA Most Valuable Player as the team again won the NBA title. At this time, his play reached such a level of excellence that many regarded him as the greatest player of all time. Larry followed all this up by winning two more NBA MVP awards in 1985 and in 1986 when the Celtics added still another NBA title.

Larry Bird was the ultimate team player. He focused on assists, steals, and rebounding to go along with his exceptional scoring skills. He was truly the all-around player. In one way or another he would find a way to win. Dedication and hard work provided his foundation. Clearly, Larry Bird was one of the greatest and most dominant basketball players of all time.

JULIUS ERVING

Julius Erving is a basketball legend. He is remembered as the original master of the slam-dunk. Julius was a prolific scorer and rebounder. He scored over 30,000 points in his professional career and is one of only the very few players in the history of the game to achieve this feat. Currently, Julius is enshrined in the Basketball Hall of Fame.

Recognition of Julius began in high school where he competed on all-county and all-Long Island teams. Because of his superior performances in the classroom as well as on the court, he was nicknamed "the Doctor." His teammates would later alter this to "Dr. J." After high school, Julius broke freshman records at the University of Massachusetts for scoring and rebounding while leading his team to an undefeated season. The next year he had the second best rebound tally in the country. He joined the NCAA All-Star team and was voted most valuable player on the tour. Julius left the university to play professional basketball in his junior year. He left as one of only seven players in the history of NCAA basketball to average over 20 points and 20 rebounds per game.

In 1971, Julius began his professional career with the Virginia Squires of the American Basketball Association. He was named ABA Rookie of the Year and led the ABA in scoring the following year with 31.9 points per game. Because of a complicated legal wrangle over his contract, he moved on to the New York Nets after an out-of-court settlement. Again, Julius led the league in scoring and the Nets to an ABA championship. In the first game of the championship series, he scored 47 points, sparking comparisons with the greatest players of all time. The following year, he would score 57 points in a single game against San Diego.

After being voted Most Valuable Player in the ABA from 1974 to 1976, Julius became a Philadelphia 76er in the National Basketball Association. In his 11 years with the 76ers, he led the team to an NBA championship in 1983 and continued to establish himself as one of the game's greatest players. The incredible performances of Julius Erving are fixed in the memories of everyone who ever saw him play.

MICHAEL JORDAN

Michael played his college ball at North Carolina. He was named the Atlantic Coast Conference Rookie of the Year for his freshman year. Michael's most impressive moment was when he hit a jump shot that made North Carolina NCAA champions. During this time, he became the premiere college player in the country. Awards included being named an All-American and the *Sporting News* selected him twice as college player of the year.

After college, the Chicago Bulls chose Michael and offered him a multi-year contract. He was an immediate success, was chosen as NBA Rookie of the Year and selected as a starter in the All-Star game. Against the Boston Celtics in the 1986 playoffs, he averaged 43.7 points a game in the three-game series and set a playoff record by scoring 63 points in a single game. The next season, Michael became only the second player to score 3,000 points in a season. In the 1987–88 season, he received a number of honors that included the NBA's Most Valuable Player and NBA Defensive Player of the Year awards. Michael was an all-court player and was the first to win both the scoring title and defensive award in the same season. As the Bulls won the 1991 NBA title, he had won his fifth consecutive scoring title. Over the years, Michael has proven himself to be one of the greatest basketball players of all time.

Mark Price

Mark Price was one of the most accurate shooters in college and professional basketball history. He is a four-time All-Star and has been named four times to the All-NBA Team. He was the NBA's Long Distance Shoot-out winner at All-Star Weekend for two years. Mark holds the all-time NBA record for free-throw percentage (.904).

At Georgia Tech, Mark Price completed his college career as the school's second all-time leading scorer and ranked 10th on the ACC all-time scoring list. He was an All-American during his junior and senior years and became the first freshman ever to lead the ACC in scoring, averaging 20.3 points per game. Mark entered the NBA in 1986 with the Cleveland Cavaliers.

During his 12 years in the NBA, Mark was consistently one of the top scorers in the league. He was also consistently ranked amongst its assist leaders. He has seen action in 47 playoff games, averaging over 17 points per game. He was the first Cleveland Cavalier to be nominated to the All-NBA First Team. Finally, Mark was a member of the Dream Team, the gold medal winners of the 1994 World Championship Games.

Isiah Thomas

Isiah "Zeke" Thomas was one of the finest point guards to ever play the game of basketball. Even though he was "small" (barely over six feet) he had as complete a game as anyone to ever play the game. He could shoot from the outside with the best, he could drive to the basket, and he was a great passer and a tenacious defender. The respect he earned from other players led him to be chosen president of the NBA Players' Association in the late 1980s and early 1990s. He ended his playing career as the Detroit Pistons' all-time leader in scoring, assists, steals, and games played. During his tenure in Detroit, he led the Pistons to consecutive NBA titles in '88–89 and '89–90. He twice was named the NBA's MVP and was an All-Star for 12 years in a row. He was also known as the "baby-faced assassin" in reference to the smiling demeanor that belied his toughness and competitiveness. His 46-point performance, on a severely sprained ankle, in the 1987–88 playoffs still ranks as one of the NBA's most outstanding moments. In 1997 he was named one of the league's 50 greatest players ever.

Thomas' wide range of talents served him well after his career ended. He became part owner of the Toronto Raptors and, later, owner of the CBA. Thomas, also, found he deeply missed the game of basketball and subsequently coached the Indiana Pacers.

JERRY WEST

During his three years at West Virginia, Jerry averaged 24.8 points and 13.3 rebounds a game, while shooting 50.6%. In 1958 he led West Virginia to the number one ranking in the country. He was voted Most Valuable Player all three years and went on to win a gold medal with the 1960 Olympic Team as well as being named MVP in the 1959 National Collegiate Athletic Association Final Four.

In 1961, Jerry entered professional basketball playing for the Los Angeles Lakers. In his second year he averaged 30.8 points per game. One of the highlights was a record-breaking 63-point effort against the New York Knicks. Later, Jerry averaged a career high 31.3 points per game during the 1965-66 playing season. Along with his offensive skills, his defensive skills were recognized through being selected to the NBA All-Defensive team from 1969 to 1973.

Jerry was known as "Mr. Clutch." He earned this nickname because of his uncanny ability to win numerous college and professional games in highly pressurized situations. Jerry continues to hold many of the Los Angeles Lakers' team records and was named on the NBA All-Time team in 1980, as well as being inducted into the Naismith Memorial Basketball Hall of Fame.

BOXING

Muhammad Ali

At the age of 16, Muhammad (known as Cassius Clay at that time) won Louisville's Golden Gloves light heavyweight title. Following high school, he won his second AAU title and a gold medal for the United States in the 1960 Rome Olympics. The victory at the Olympics marked his 40th consecutive win. In 1960, Cassius won his first professional fight at Louisville's Freedom Hall.

Cassius was loud and outspoken. He decided before each fight that he should announce in which round he would win the fight. Amazingly, his predictions would come true and he became known as the "Louisville Lip." Being undefeated after 19 professional fights, 15 by knockouts, Cassius finally got his chance to fight Sonny Liston for the heavyweight championship in 1964. He won convincingly and shouted to the world, "I am the king." After this win, Cassius announced that he was becoming a member of the Nation of Islam and changed his name to Muhammad Ali. Over the following years, he would defend his title nine times and had three memorable fights with Joe Frazier. The third fight with Frazier, the "Thrilla in Manila," is considered by many fight experts to be the greatest in the history of the sport.

Muhammad Ali was named and recognized as the greatest heavyweight champion of all time by *The Ring* (magazine) in 1978. He was a colorful and outspoken public figure who at times appeared larger than life. This graceful and quick fighter made such an impact on the sport of boxing that it would never be the same.

Joe Frazier

The highlight of Joe's early career came when he won an Olympic gold medal for the United States in 1964. He achieved this in spite of having a broken left hand. Joe turned professional in 1965. He won his first fight with a knockout in the first round. Of his 19 wins in less than two and a half years, only two of the fights went the distance. Joe's aggressive boxing style earned him the nickname "Smokin' Joe." He had ferocious punching power in both fists and during a fight he would just keep coming forward, relentlessly putting pressure on his opponent.

In 1967, he won the world heavyweight crown and was later named Fighter of the Year by the Boxing Writers Association in 1969. In what was billed as the "Fight of the Century" he fought Muhammad Ali in 1971. Joe knocked Ali down in the 15th round with a terrific left hook and at the final bell became the undisputed heavyweight champion of the world.

Joe was inducted into *The Ring*'s Boxing Hall of Fame in 1980. Twenty-seven of his 32 victories came by way of knockouts, and he possessed one of the highest knockout ratios in the history of modern boxing.

CYCLING

Karen Bliss Livingston

Karen Bliss Livingston is considered one of the world's greatest cyclists. She is a seven-time U.S. National champion (1986, '87, '89, '90, '91, '94, and '97). She has also participated in and won a number of international races. Moreover, Karen was a captain for some of the top-ranked women's teams in the United States.

In 1991, Karen was the National Prestige Classic Series champion and finished first at the Niedersachsen Stage Race in Germany. The following year she took the first-place prize at the Flevotour Road Race in the Netherlands. Over this period of time Karen was a three-time World Championship Team Member. In 1993, she won a Gold Medal at the National Track Championship Omnium and was a Silver Medallist at the Goodwill Games in St. Petersburg, Russia. Finally, at the World Road Race Championships in Spain, Karen was the top placed American (sixth overall).

Karen Bliss Livingston has excelled as both an individual and a team participant. She has more than 230 career wins. In 1997 she was named U.S. Cycling Athlete of the Year. Karen has set the bar very high and has taken her place among the outstanding athletes of our time.

FOOTBALL

Jim Brown

At Syracuse University, Jim made All-American and set a major college record by scoring 43 points (six touchdowns and seven extra points in a single game). During his collegiate career (1954–56) he compiled 2,091 total yards, 25 touchdowns, and 187 points. The Cleveland Browns selected Jim in the first round of the 1957 NFL draft.

With Cleveland, Jim established NFL records for the following categories: most seasons leading the NFL in rushing, consecutive years leading the NFL in rushing, career rushing attempts, career rushing yards, games with more than 100 yards rushing, career yardage average per game, rushing touchdowns in a season, lifetime rushing touchdowns, and rushing yards in one season. He was named the NFL's Most Valuable Player in 1958 and 1965 and played in three NFL championship games. An All-NFL selection eight years, Jim was named to the Pro Bowl every year of his career.

In 1971, Jim Brown was elected to the Pro Football Hall of Fame. As a great running back, he demonstrated power, speed, and quickness, and although many opponents hit him hard, he never missed an NFL game and was seldom stopped. Jim Brown is widely regarded as the toughest and most powerful running back in the history of the NFL.

STEVE KINER

Steve Kiner graduated from Hillsborough High School (Tampa, FL) in 1966 and went on to play at the University of Tennessee from 1966 to 1969. With the Vols, he was named Sophomore of the Year in the SEC in 1967, All-SEC in '67, '68, and '69, Defensive Player of the Year in the SEC in '68 and '69, and Consensus All-American in 1968 and '69. Steve was ninth on the Heisman Ballot in 1969 while Tennessee won the SEC Championship in 1967 and 1969. He was drafted by the Dallas Cowboys in 1970.

Early on Steve played an important part in helping the Cowboys make it to the Super Bowl in 1971. He later excelled as linebacker for the New England Patriots and Houston Oilers and returned to the Super Bowl with the Washington Redskins. In addition, Steve played in 12 divisional or conference championship games. During the course of his tenure in the NFL, while playing for the Patriots, he was named Defensive MVP and nominated to the All-Pro Team.

Steve Kiner was presented the Dick Butkus Award given to one of football's most outstanding linebackers. Further recognition was given to Steve when he was elected to the College Football Hall of Fame in 1998. Overall, Steve Kiner was a fierce competitor and, pound for pound, arguably one of the game's greatest linebackers.

JOE MONTANA

Joe attended Notre Dame in 1974. As a quarterback for the Fighting Irish, he was known as "the Comeback Kid" for his heroics in a number of memorable games. In 1975, Joe brought the team back from a 14-6 fourth-quarter deficit against North Carolina to a 21-14 win. Even more dramatically, he erased a 30-10 deficit with three touchdown passes in the second half against the Air Force Academy. In 1977, Joe took the Fighting Irish to the Cotton Bowl and beat previously undefeated Texas 38-10. At season's end, Notre Dame was voted the number-one team in the country.

The San Francisco 49ers drafted Joe in 1979. With San Francisco from 1982 to 1989, he established himself as the premier quarterback in the National Football League (NFL) by setting numerous records and leading his team to three Super Bowl victories. His records included highest passing efficiency rating in a season, highest completion percentage in a postseason game, most touchdown passes in a Super Bowl game, and most yards passing in a Super Bowl game. He was selected NFL Player of the Year in 1989 and placed on the NFL Pro Bowl Team in 1982, '84, '85, '86, and '89.

Joe Montana has endured injury and adversity with a special kind of poise. He has demonstrated a unique form of motivation that included challenge and a "never-say-die" attitude. Joe has certainly earned the title of superstar and is rightfully considered as one of the great quarterbacks of all time.

Joe Namath

At the University of Alabama, sophomore Joe Namath led a senior team to a 10-1 record. His senior year with the Crimson Tide was his best. Despite knee problems, Joe played brilliantly while leading his team to the National Championship in 1964. After the season-ending Orange Bowl game, Joe became the first big-money free agent. The New York Jets were willing to pay the money because their owner was sure that "Broadway Joe" would bring victory and glamour to his team.

Joe began his professional career in 1966. He passed for five touchdowns in his first home game with the Jets. In 1967, Joe set a professional football record by passing for 4,007 yards. In 1968, he led the Jets to the Eastern Division title. Before the Super Bowl, he surprisingly guaranteed a Jet victory over the heavily favored Baltimore Colts. In that game, Joe shocked the sports world by directing a stunning 16-7 upset win over the mighty Colts. After the Super Bowl, he became the biggest celebrity to hit New York since Babe Ruth.

When operating at his full potential, Joe Namath could be considered as the best quarterback in the history of professional football. He was awesome with the strength and accuracy of his arm as well as his unusually fast drop-back into the pocket. Finally, Joe earned the respect of players and fans with his ability to absorb punishment and bounce back from injuries.

RAY NITSCHKE

Early in his career, Ray made All-State as a quarterback in high school. Following high school, he chose the University of Illinois where he played quarterback and fullback. Ray played in both the Senior Bowl and College All-Star game with the Fighting Illini. After graduation in 1958, the Green Bay Packers drafted him.

Ray took over the starting spot as the Packer's middle linebacker in his first year. In this position, he could show his skills as a hard-hitting lineman. By 1962, he had become one of football's most feared tacklers. His rugged defensive play against both the run and the pass made the opposition tentative and concerned. Ray became defensive captain and led Lombardi's great Green Bay Packer teams to five National Football League titles and Super Bowl victories. Known for his ferocious hitting and tackling ability, he played the key role on what was considered one of the most invincible linebacking units in NFL history. Ray made All-Pro from 1964 through 1966, played in the 1965 Pro Bowl, and was named most valuable player in the1962 title game.

Following his retirement, Ray was named to the AFL-NFL 1960-84 All-Star Team, as well as to the NFL All-Pro Team for the decade of the '60s. In 1962, the NFL honored him as their all-time top linebacker. Finally, in 1978, he was elected to the Pro Football Hall of Fame.

DEION SANDERS

Deion attended Florida State University, where he excelled in football, track, and baseball. He was selected by the New York Yankees in 1988 and played with their Columbus triple-A club. After signing with the Atlanta Falcons professional football team, Deion became a two-sport athlete. In 1989, he became the first athlete ever to hit a home run and run for a touchdown, all in the same week. He was later signed by the Atlanta Braves as a free agent in 1991 and helped lead the Braves into the World Series. In 1992, he became the first player in major league history to lead the major leagues in triples despite having played in fewer than 100 games. Deion was traded to the Cincinnati Reds in 1994 and was declared "most exciting player" and "fastest baserunner" by *Baseball America*.

Deion signed with the San Francisco 49ers in September of 1994. He was named Associated Press Defensive Player of the Year while helping to lead the 49ers to a Super Bowl victory. His baseball career continued after a trade to the San Francisco Giants in 1995 where he hit .285, posted a .444 slugging percentage, and ranked third in the national league in triples. After signing with the Dallas Cowboys of the National Football League for the 1995 season, he promptly contributed to yet another Super Bowl victory.

In 1996, he played both offense and defense for the Cowboys. He ranked second on the team with 475 receiving yards and first on the club in fumble recoveries. Deion earned his fifth trip to the Pro Bowl as a cornerback, was named All-Pro by the Associated Press, and became the first full-time, two-way player in the NFL since Chuck Bednarik.

Speed and agility was the name of Deion's game. NFL quarterbacks were very reluctant to throw to Deion's side of the field. As a baseball player, he had many of the attributes of an ideal lead-off hitter, and he was a winner. As a "team mover," he added one of the most important intangibles to a team's success. There have been few players in the history of sport with the versatility of a Deion Sanders.

Y. A. TITTLE

Y. A. was one of the finest college quarterbacks of his time. He gained All-Southeastern Conference honors in his junior and senior seasons and led Louisiana State University to the 1946 Cotton Bowl. Following his college career, the Cleveland Browns of the All America Football Conference selected him in the NFL draft.

After the AAFC folded, Y.A. joined the San Francisco 49ers of the NFL. In 1952, he took over as starting quarterback and kept the job for the next 8 years. His best year with the 49ers was 1957, when he led the team to a first place tie for the Western Conference title. Y.A. combined with receiver R. C. Owens to produce the famous alley-oop pass that helped the 49ers win several games. At the end of the year, he was chosen for the All-NFL team.

In 1961, Y.A. was traded to the New York Giants. He quickly led the Giants to three straight Eastern Conference Championships from 1961 to 1963. He passed for an incredible 93 touchdown passes during those seasons and was chosen as the NFL Player of the Year in 1962 and 1963. Y.A. is known as the greatest quarterback in New York Giants history, and Giants coach Allie Sherman called him the greatest quarterback he had ever seen. He was a tremendous competitor, fearless under pressure, and achieved his greatest success at an age when most football players are finished. Y.A. was selected to the Pro Football Hall of Fame in 1971.

CHARLIE TRIPPI

Charlie led the powerful University of Georgia Bulldogs to a win in the 1943 Rose Bowl. He was selected the game's Most Valuable Player. After returning from military service, he sparked the Bulldogs to an undefeated season in 1946. Charlie became a unanimous selection to the All-America team and also won the Maxwell Award for the nation's best college player.

Charlie was known as "Triple Threat" Trippi because of his superb running, accurate passing, and strong punting. He also played defensive safety and his coach called him the best tackler he had ever seen. His versatility extended to other sports. He was a great baseball player and was selected to the baseball All-America team in 1946.

Charlie entered professional football in 1947 with the Chicago Cardinals. In his first year, he led the Cardinals to the NFL Championship. During the nine seasons with the Cardinals, he set records in rushing, punt return average, touchdowns, and punting average. Charlie accumulated more than 7,000 yards and averaged almost 50 yards per punt in his professional career. His coach called him the greatest player he had ever coached.

Charlie could do it all on the football field. He was one of the last triple-threat players and one of the best. Charlie Trippi's greatness was recognized in 1968 with his induction into the Pro Football Hall of Fame.

JOHNNY UNITAS

Johnny was drafted out of the University of Louisville by the Pittsburgh Steelers in 1955 and eventually found himself with the Baltimore Colts in 1956. In 1957, he led the NFL in passing yardage with 2,550 yards and in touchdown passes with 24. In 1958, Johnny led the Colts to the NFL Championship with a sudden death victory over the New York Giants. Sportswriters have called it the greatest game ever played. The following year, the Colts again won the NFL Championship. In 1970, burdened by numerous injuries, he came back and led the Colts to victory in the Super Bowl.

Johnny continued setting records as a quarterback. From 1956 to 1960, he set a record by throwing at least one touchdown pass in 47 consecutive games. By the time he retired, he held the NFL records for the most pass attempts, most completions, most yardage, most 300-yard games, and most touchdown passes.

Johnny won the NFL's Most Valuable Player award in 1959, '64, and '67. He was named All-Pro in 1957, '58, '64, '65, '66, and '67. In 1970,

he was named the NFL Player of the Decade by the Associated Press and
was named to the Pro Football Hall of Fame in 1979. Johnny Unitas,
always determined and rarely losing his composure, proved himself to be
one of the greatest quarterbacks of all time.

GOLF

NANCY LOPEZ

Nancy was an immediate sensation in college. The Tulsa women's golf
team entered nine tournaments in the 1975-76 season and won six of
them. Nancy was the individual winner in six of the tournaments, won the
national championship as an individual, and was All-American both years.
Following college, she joined the Ladies' Professional Golf Association
(LPGA) as a touring professional in 1977.

Nancy's first year on the tour was one of the most remarkable for any
athlete in any sport. At the age of 21, she won nine tournaments including
five in a row. In addition, Nancy set records for the amount of prize
money won in one year and had the lowest scoring average. She was unanimously named both Rookie of the Year and Player of the Year. This was a
feat never equaled in professional golf. Her second year was as successful as
the first, winning eight tournaments and again being selected Player of the
Year. Nancy elevated her status from golf super-star to sports legend and
brought women's golf to a new level. In the following years, she continued
her success and won enough tournaments to qualify for the Hall of Fame.

Nancy Lopez may be the best woman golfer of all time. She is the person most responsible for the success of the LPGA. Aside from her superior
performances, Nancy combined her tremendous athletic ability and warm
personality into being an effective role model for young people.

JACK NICKLAUS

At Ohio State, Jack won the U.S. Amateur Championship twice and
was the runner-up to Arnold Palmer by two strokes in the 1960 U.S.
Open. Following college, he turned professional in 1961. In his first year
as a professional he played in 26 United States events. Along with his win
at the U.S. Open, he also won the Seattle Open, Portland Open, and the
World Series of Golf. For all this, Jack was nominated Rookie of the Year.

Through the 1990 season, Jack had won more than 90 tournaments
worldwide. He was second on the all-time tournament winners list, with

70 PGA tour victories. He had the lowest career scoring average (approximately 70.5) and led the PGA tour in career earnings for a number of years. Jack has won 20 "majors" and finished second 19 times. This will be a record to be contended with for decades.

Jack Nicklaus is a legend. He is arguably the greatest golfer to ever play the game. His records and list of achievements on the golf course will set a standard for others to measure themselves in the generations ahead.

ARNOLD PALMER

Arnold's odd swing and daring strategy made him very popular. He attracted enormous galleries whenever and wherever he played. His fans were nicknamed "Arnie's Army." His popularity was not simply because of his dashing style and personable nature. He was in fact one of the greatest golfers of his time.

Arnold's first major victory was the 1958 Masters Tournament. He won the tournament by a single shot. Even more memorable was his victory at the same tournament in 1960. He sank two long putts on the 17th and 18th holes to give him an exciting come-from-behind win. Arnold had a knack for coming from behind when he was seemingly out of contention. These late charges in the final round were one of the attractions that his fans looked forward to.

Arnold Palmer was a dominant golfer in the 1960s. During that time, he won the U.S. Open, two British Opens, and a fourth Masters. Arnold continued to win tournaments until 1973. His daring style and widespread popularity helped to establish golf as a major spectator sport. Arnold was recognized as the foremost golfer of the period from 1958 to 1965.

GARY PLAYER

In 1959, Gary Player became the youngest player to win the British Open since 1868. After that win, he made a determined effort to succeed on the American Tour. In 1961, he won the Masters Tournament and was the leading money winner on the tour. Gary then proceeded to win the four major tournaments of the Grand Slam of Golf: the British Open, U.S. Open, the PGA Championship, and the Masters. Gary Player, along with Jack Nicklaus and Arnold Palmer, was considered part of the "Big Three" of international golf during the 1960s. Although he did not win every tournament, Gary was consistently among the highest money winners.

After winning the PGA Championship for a second time, he underwent a serious operation that made it impossible for him to play for more than a year. However, Gary bounced back from his illness with victories in the British Open and the Masters in 1974. At the end of each tournament, he would play a special round to correct his mistakes. He also worked on increasing his physical strength with exercise and diet and was one of the first to insist that golf was a game that required athletic training.

Overall, Gary won nine major tournament titles and more than 129 tournaments around the world. He was the youngest player to win the British Open, the oldest to win the Masters, and the first player from outside the United States to top the money list for the American Tour. Considering all of his impressive career achievements, Gary Player was truly an exceptional performer in the world of golf.

HOCKEY

BERNARD GEOFFRION

Born in Montreal, Quebec, Bernard Geoffrion commenced his hockey career in the National Hockey League in 1951, earning his nickname, "Boom Boom," for his powerful slap shot, developed while playing junior hockey for the Laval Nationale. Following his teammate, "Rocket" Richard, he was the second player in the NHL to score 50 goals in one season. As left-wing to Montreal's superstar front line with Maurice Richard and Jean Beliveau, Geoffrion was on board the Canadiens team for six Stanley Cup Championships. He won the Art Ross Trophy as league-scoring champion in 1955. Geoffrion passed away in Atlanta in 2006 after acting as the first coach for the newly formed Atlanta Thrashers.

WAYNE GRETZKY

In 1978, Wayne turned professional and joined the Indianapolis Racers of the World Hockey Association at the age of 17. The Racers then sold him to the Edmonton Oilers, who presented him with a five-million-dollar, 20-year contract. At 18 years old, Wayne showed tremendous promise. In 1980, he became the youngest player to score 50 goals in a season. Sportswriters awarded this young superstar two major hockey honors: the first of nine Most Valuable Player awards he would receive over 10 years, as well as the league's most gentlemanly player award. The *Sporting News* named him athlete of the Year in 1981. Wayne led the Oilers to four Stanley Cups between 1984 and 1988. Wayne Gretzky had become a national hero. Thirteen songs were written about "The Great Gretzky."

The Oilers sold Wayne to the Los Angeles Kings for 18 million dollars in 1988. With the Kings, he won the Hart Memorial Trophy as the NHL's MVP. In 1989, Wayne made headlines when he broke Gordie Howe's NHL career scoring record. At that time, Wayne also went on to win his eighth NHL scoring title.

Wayne Gretzky was a polite and serious superstar with superb grace and speed on the ice. Training from the time he was a toddler, he had continuously broken records throughout his career. Many have called him the most valuable player in the history of hockey. His exceptional performances with the Edmonton Oilers as well as the Los Angeles Kings strongly support such claims.

GORDIE HOWE

During the 1949 Stanley Cup playoffs, Gordie began to emerge as a star with the Detroit Red Wings. He had top points in the 11 games, with eight goals and three assists. The following season, Gordie became the league's third-highest scorer. In 1950, he reached a major milestone in his career, not only scoring his 100th goal, but also replacing the great Maurice Richard of the Montreal Canadiens at right wing position for the First Team All-Stars.

Gordie was a superb stick handler and was very strong. He was capable of sending a puck flying at 120 miles per hour with a flick of his wrists. He played aggressive, tough hockey that opponents feared and respected. Gordie's 545th goal in 1963 broke the all-time record of Maurice Richard. Not counting playoff goals, he scored 801 goals in his NHL career, a record that would hold for many years.

Gordie Howe is the standard by which many hockey players measure themselves and their achievements. He endured as an outstanding professional hockey player for thirty-two seasons, a record that will not easily be broken. Known as "Mister Hockey," Gordie Howe is regarded by many as the best hockey player of all time.

JUDO

DOUG ROGERS

Starting judo at the age of 16 at Outremont High School in Montreal, Canada, Doug then moved to Japan at 19 where he trained for five years at the Kodokan School of Judo in Tokyo and Metropolitan Police Dojo. A strapping judo-ka at six feet, four inches, he won the Silver Medal in the heavyweight category of the 1964 Tokyo Olympics, and the following year he took the Bronze Medal at the World Judo Championships in Rio de Janeiro and a Gold Medal at the Pan American Judo Championships in Guatemala. That year he was the first Caucasian ever to compete in the Japanese National Championships and was honored to receive the "Top Fighter" Award. In 1967, at the Pan Am Games in Winnipeg, he won the Gold Medal in the open-weight category and the Silver in the heavyweight category.

Despite a serious injury in the 1972 Olympics in Munich, Doug came out fourth in the open category. He is featured in "100 Year History of Japanese Judo." In 2007 he was inducted into the Canadian Black Belt Hall of Fame.

TENNIS

Jimmy Connors

Attending the University of California at Los Angeles (UCLA) in 1970-71, Jimmy won the National Collegiate Athletic Association (NCAA) Championship. He was the first freshman ever to win an NCAA title. A few years later, Jimmy competed in Jacksonville, Florida, as a professional. He won his first tournament as a professional and continued to win others. He quickly became the hottest player on the circuit.

In 1972, Jimmy made the Davis Cup Team, representing the United States. He played in his first Wimbledon that same year and had 75 victories, the highest total among All-American male professionals. The year 1974 was perhaps Jimmy's best. He won 99 of 103 matches. Included were Wimbledon, the U.S. Open, and the Australian Open titles. Between 1974 and 1978, he was known as the most consistent player in men's tennis. During this time, Jimmy won more than 50 tournaments, and in 1984 became the first player to win 100 singles titles.

Jimmy Connors' style of play was always attacking, intense concentration, crisp ground strokes, great return of service, and precision timing, and behind all this was an intense burning, competitive fire. Along with the many accomplishments, the intensity and drive will always be remembered as an intrinsic part of the personality that made up this great tennis player.

CHRIS EVERT

Chris won her first singles tournament at the age of 10. She had an excellent baseline game and was so controlled on the court that she was called such names as "Little Miss Cool" and the "Ice Maiden." In 1970, Chris won her first major tournament at the age of 15. She defeated Margaret Court, who was ranked number one in the world. Following this win, she competed on the U.S. team that won the 1971 Wightman Cup and later participated in her first U.S. Open, where she established herself as a player who would help to change women's tennis forever.

Chris turned professional at the age of 17. In 1974, she won her first Wimbledon and was ranked number one in the world from 1974 to 1978 and 1980 to 1981. Overall, Chris won 18 Grand Slam singles titles: Wimbledon three times, and the U.S. Open five times. Finally, in 1989, she won five straight Federation Cup matches and helped the U.S. team win the competition in Tokyo.

Chris Evert was a super-athlete because she was motivated and controlled and had excellent concentration and consistent strokes. Few players in the history of tennis have performed as skillfully and successfully for so many consecutive years. Chris will always be remembered as one of the greatest women's tennis players of all time.

TRACK

JOAN BENOIT

Joan attended North Carolina State University on a track scholarship. At this time, she made the women's All-American track team and led her team to a second place finish in the national championship. Before leaving college, Joan had begun entering races on her own. For the most part, she competed in 10,000-meter road races and ran the women's world's fastest time in one of those races.

In 1979, Joan won the Boston Marathon. She took the lead on Heartbreak Hill and steadily pulled ahead, finishing first in 2 hours, 35 minutes, and 15 seconds, the fastest marathon ever run by an American woman. However, soon after that victory, her career as a runner nearly ended. Continuing foot pain forced her to have surgery. After a quick recovery, Joan ran a marathon, almost 2 minutes faster than the existing American women's record. This was followed by an outstanding performance in the 1983 Boston Marathon, when she finished first in 2 hours, 22 minutes, and 43 seconds, almost three minutes faster than the world's record for women.

Seventeen days before the American Olympic trials Joan had orthroscopic surgery on her right knee. Many doubted that she would have a chance against her healthy, well-trained opponents. The first Olympic women's marathon was held in 1984 at Los Angeles. Although she was not the favorite, she took the lead after the first three miles and finished more than a minute ahead of her nearest competitor. Although this victory was to be the peak of her career, she later set a new women's marathon world record of 2 hours, 21 minutes, and 21 seconds in 1985. These achievements reflect the incredible determination and dedication of a super-athlete and one of the greatest runners in the history of distance running.

MICHAEL JOHNSON

Michael is considered by some as the best runner of the 20th century. He became the only male to ever win both the 200- and 400-meter gold medals in the same Olympiad when he stunned the world in Atlanta in 1996. He is also the only man to simultaneously hold the world record for both events (19.32 and 43.18 seconds). If anything, Michael was a testimony to consistency. He won five world championships (four at 400 meters and one at 200 meters) and anchored numerous world championship and world record-setting relay teams over a 10-year period. He is the only man in history to win nine career gold medals at the world championships.

A good, but not exceptional, high school performer, he blossomed under the tutelage of Clyde Hart at Baylor University. Suffering more than his share of injuries, Michael demonstrated the mental toughness to keep coming back and raising the level of his performances. His air of confidence before and during competition have earned him the nickname "Michael Cool."

JEARL MILES

Jearl's senior year in high school was a breakthrough season. During this season, the NCAA had placed her third in the 400 and eighth in the long jump. She also took third in the USA\MOBILE 400 and seventh in the Olympic Trials 400. This all earned her first *Track and Field News* ranking of number seven in the United States. Graduating in 1988 from Alabama A&M, Jearl was on her way.

In 1989, she moved up to number five in the United States, while scoring a second at the USA\MOBILE, a third at the Olympic Festival, and a second at the World University Games. She continued to hold that ranking in 1990, finishing fifth at USA\MOBILE and winning the Olympic Festival 400. In 1991, Jearl took second in the USA\MOBILE 400, won a bronze medal in the Pan American Games, took fifth in the World Championships in Tokyo, and burned fast relay legs in Havana (49.9 seconds) and in Tokyo (49.24 seconds). For the year, Jearl was ranked number two in the United States and number five in the world by *Track and Field News*. Then in 1993, she scored a runaway victory for her first USA\MOBILE Championship, and a couple of months later in Stuttgart, Jearl ran the race of her life to win the World Championship in 49.82 seconds, which earned her the number one world ranking.

After winning the Goodwill Games title in St. Petersburg, Russia, in 1994, Jearl began the 1995 season undefeated with five consecutive 400-meter victories on the new U.S. indoor circuit. She topped all this off with a new USA\MOBILE meet record in the 400. The time of 50.99 seconds was the fastest indoor 400 ever run on American soil. This made her one of the fastest American indoor runners ever. Jearl Miles, Olympian and World Champion, is one of the great athletes in the history of track and field.

Jim Ryun

In high school, Jim won the state championship by running a 4-minute, 26.4-second mile. He continued to improve and had dropped his time to 4 minutes, 1.7 seconds, 2 seconds faster than the previous record. In the Compton Invitational Meet at age 17, Jim became the first high school runner to ever run a sub-four-minute mile. Finally, while still in high school, he qualified for the 1964 Olympic team. In 1965, Jim defeated the Olympic champion, Peter Snell, by running a new American record of 3 minutes, 55.3 seconds.

Then, on July 17, 1966, in Berkeley, California, it finally happened. Jim blistered the track, setting a new world record for the mile of 3 minutes, 51.3 seconds. He was then voted the world's most outstanding athlete by 54 sports editors in 23 countries. In addition, he received the James E. Sullivan Award for being the best amateur athlete, as well as being named Sportsman of the Year by *Sports Illustrated*. In the following years, Jim continued to set records, lowering his own world mark to 3 minutes, 51.1 seconds and setting yet another world mark for the 1,500 meters at 3 minutes, 33.1 seconds. Later, in 1968, Jim won a Silver Medal at the Olympics in Mexico City.

Jim was focused on being the best. He had an incredible inner drive that was reflected in twice-a-day workouts that were awesome. He would sometimes run 40 repeat quarter-mile distances in the intense Kansas heat or 16 miles in the rain. His dedication to his goals was extraordinary by any standard. Jim Ryun was truly a super-athlete.

NOTES

PREFACE

1. M. Ali, *The Greatest* (New York: Random House, 1975).

2. The material in this chapter is drawn from an interview with Jack Nicklaus.

3. The material in this chapter is drawn from an interview with Bernard "Boom Boom" Geoffrion.

4. M. Gladwell, *Blink: The Power of Thinking without Thinking* (Boston, MA: Little, Brown, 2005).

5. The material in this chapter is drawn from an interview with Brad Wilkerson.

6. D. Karnazes, *Ultramarathon Man: Confessions of an All Night Runner* (New York: Penguin, 2006).

INTRODUCTION

1. The material in this chapter is drawn from an interview with Jack Nicklaus.

2. The material in this chapter is drawn from an interview with Ted Williams.

3. The material in this chapter is drawn from interview with Mario Andretti.

4. The material in this chapter is drawn from an interview with Gordie Howe.

CHAPTER 2: BIG GOALS

1. Quotations 1 and 3–9 were taken from interviews by the authors with the individual athletes.

2. Taken from books by and about Michael Jordan: M. Jordan, *Rare Air* (San Francisco, CA: Collins Publishers, 1993); M. Jordan, *I Can't Accept Not Trying* (San Francisco, CA: Harper, 1994); M. Vancil, ed., *Driven from Within: Michael Jordan* (New York: Atria Books, 2005).

CHAPTER 4: LITTLE GOALS: THE AIM IN COMPETITION

1. The material in this chapter is drawn from an interview with Michael Jordan.

CHAPTER 5: RESULTS AND PROCESS

1. The material in this chapter is drawn from an interview with Steve Kiner.

CHAPTER 8: WHAT THE SUPER-ATHLETES SAY ABOUT CONFIDENCE

1. The material in this chapter is drawn from interviews the authors conducted with the many athletes.

CHAPTER 9: WHEN CONFIDENCE IS LACKING … HOW TO BUILD IT

1. The material in this chapter on Michael Jordan was drawn from books by and about Michael Jordan: M. Jordan, *Rare Air* (San Francisco, CA: Collins Publishers, 1993); M. Jordan, *I Can't Accept Not Trying* (San Francisco, CA: Harper, 1994); M. Vancil, ed., *Driven from Within: Michael Jordan* (New York: Atria Books, 2005).
2. The material in this chapter is drawn from an interview with Matt Williams.
3. The material in this chapter is drawn from an interview with Jack Nicklaus.
4. The material in this chapter is drawn from an interview with Jim Brown.

CHAPTER 10: PUTTING CONFIDENCE TO WORK

1. The material in this chapter is drawn from an interview with Jim Brown.
2. The material in this chapter is drawn from an interview with Richard Petty.

CHAPTER 12: WHAT SUPER-ATHLETES SAY ABOUT CONCENTRATION

1. Quotations 1–10 and 12–19 were taken from interviews by the authors with the individual athletes.
2. C. Evert and N. Amdur, *Chrissie: My Own Story* (New York: Simon & Schuster, 1982).

CHAPTER 13: BROAD AND NARROW ATTENTION

1. Taken from an interview with Hal McRae.

CHAPTER 20: APPLYING THE FOCUS EDGE MINDSET

1. Taken from an interview with Barry Larkin.
2. Taken from an interview with Matt Williams.
3. Taken from an interview with Mark Davis.

BIBLIOGRAPHY

Aaron, H., and F. Bisher. *Hank Aaron, R. F.: The Story of My Life, the Good Times and the Bad, from Mobile to Milwaukee to Atlanta.* Cleveland, OH: World Publishing Co., 1969.

Ali, M. *The Greatest.* New York: Random House, 1975.

Baldwin, S. C., J. B. Jenkins, and H. Aaron. *Bad Henry.* Radnor, PA: Chilton, 1974.

Barkley, C., and R. Johnson. *Outrageous.* New York: Avon Books, 1992.

Barrell, J.J., D. Medeiros, J.E. Barrell, and D. Price. "The Causes and Treatment of Performance Anxiety: An Experiential Approach." *Journal of Humanistic Psychology* 25(2) (Spring 1985): 106–22.

Benoit, J., and S. Baker. *Running Tide.* New York: Alfred A. Knopf, 1987.

Bird, L., and B. Ryan. *Larry Bird: Drive—The Story of My Life.* New York: Doubleday, 1989.

Brown, J., and S. Delsohn. *Out of Bounds.* New York: Zebra Books, Kensington, 1989.

Canfield, J. *The Success Principles.* New York: Harper Collins, 2005.

Conklin, T. *Muhammad Ali: The Fight for Respect.* Brookfield, CT: Millbrook Press, 1992.

Csikszentmihalyi, M. *Flow: The Psychology of Optimal Experience.* New York: Harper & Row, 1990.

Custance, C. "How Can He Get Any Better?" *Atlanta Journal-Constitution*; Atlanta, GA, November 11, 2007, F1 and F3.

Evert, C., and N. Amdur, *Chrissie: My Own Story.* New York: Simon & Schuster, 1982.

Garrity, J. "Tiger 2.0." *Sports Illustrated* 106 (April 2, 2007): 71.

Gladwell, M. *Blink: The Power of Thinking without Thinking.* Boston: Little, Brown, 2005.

Gretzky, W., and R. Reilly. *Gretzky: An Autobiography.* New York: Edward Burlington Book/Harper Collins Publishers, 1990.

Hollander, Z., and H. Bock, eds. *The Complete Encyclopedia of Ice Hockey.* Englewood Cliffs, NJ: Prentice-Hall, 1974.

Jones, C. *What Makes Winners Win.* Secaucus, NJ: Carol Publishing Group, 1997.

Jones, T. *The Great Gretzky.* Chicago, IL: Contemporary Books, 1982.

Jordan, M. *I Can't Accept Not Trying.* San Francisco, CA: Harper, 1994.

Jordan, M. *Rare Air.* San Francisco, CA: Collins Publishers, 1993.

Levine, L.D. *The Making of an American Sports Legend: Bird.* New York: McGraw Hill Book Co., 1988.

Linn, E. *Hitter: The Life and Turmoils of Ted Williams.* New York: Harcourt Brace, 1993.

Karnazes, D. *Ultramarathon Man: Confessions of an All Night Runner.* New York: Penguin, 2006.

Mantle, M. 1985 interview aired on National Public Radio's *Fresh Air,* October 16, 2007.

Mays, W., and L. Sahadi. *Say Hey: The Autobiography of Willie Mays.* New York: Simon & Schuster, 1988.

McCallum, J. "Michael: Sportsman of the Year." *Sports Illustrated* 75 (December 23, 1991): 66–81.

Moore, K. "Sprinting Into the Future." *Sports Illustrated* 85(27) (December 30, 1996-January 6, 1997): 82–83.

Moore, K. "The Man [Michael Johnson]." *Sports Illustrated* 85(7) (August 12, 1996): 26–32.

Murphy, M., and R. White. *In the Zone.* New York: Penguin Books, 1995.

Namath, J., and D. Shoop. *I Can't Wait Until Tomorrow 'Cause I Get Better Looking Every Day.* New York: Random House, 1969.

Newhan, R. "The Mystique of Sandy Koufax." *Athlon Baseball* Nashville, TN: Athlon Sports Communications, 1994.

Nicklaus, J., and K. Bowden. *On and Off the Fairway.* New York: Simon & Schuster, 1978.

Nicklaus, J., and H. Wind. *The Greatest Game of All.* New York: Simon & Schuster, 1969.

Palmer, A. *Play Great Golf.* Garden City, NY: Doubleday & Co., 1987.

Plaschke, B. with T. Lasorda. *I Live for This!* Boston, MA: Houghton Mifflin, 2007.

Price, D.D., J.E. Barrell, and J.J. Barrell. "A Quantitative-Experiential Analysis of Human Emotions." *Motivation and Emotion* 9(1) (1985): 19–38.

Raber, T. *Joe Montana: Comeback Quarterback.* Minneapolis, MN: Lerner Publications, 1989.

Ruth, B., and B. Considine, *The Babe Ruth Story.* New York: A Signet Book, Penguin, 1992.

Ryback, D. *Putting Emotional Intelligence to Work.* Woburn, MA: Butterworth-Heinemann, 1998.

St. Martin, T., and F. Frangie. *The Art of Shooting Baskets.* Chicago, IL: Contemporary Books, 1992.

Stough, C., D.H. Saklofske, and K. Hansen, eds. *Emotional Intelligence International Symposium 2005.* Croydon, Victoria, Australia: Tertiary Press, 2006.

Sugiura, K. "Gone About Going" [Dean Karnazes], *Atlanta Journal-Constitution,* Atlanta, GA, March 25, 2005, E1 and E6.

Telander, R. "Driven [Michael Jordan]." *Sports Illustrated* 85(20) (November 11, 1996).

Thottam, J. "Thank God It's Monday." *Time* 165(3), January 17, 2005.

Underwood, T. "Going Fishing with the Kid [Ted Williams]." *Sports Illustrated* 81 (July 4, 1994): 56–66.

Vancil, M., ed. *Driven from Within: Michael Jordan.* New York: Atria Books, 2005.

Watson, J.C., II, J. Lubker, A.J. Visek, and J. Geer. *Athletes' and Coaches' Perspectives of Effective Sport Psychology Consultants.* Paper Session at 115th Annual Convention of the American Psychological Association, San Francisco, August 19, 2007.

INDEX

About the Authors

JAMES J. BARRELL, Ph.D. is a professor, researcher, and consultant. With more than 25 years of experience as a consultant and human factor specialist for professional sports organizations and athletes, Barrell's affiliations have included the San Francisco Giants, San Francisco 49ers, and the Orlando Magic. He has also worked individually with numerous athletes in the NFL, NBA, major league baseball, golf, tennis, track, car racing, and professional boxing. His most recent successes include consulting on performance enhancement with the coaching staffs of the University of Florida athletic teams, playing an integral role in supporting the Gators in their 2006 and 2007 NCAA championships. As an educator and researcher, Barrell has been affiliated with the University of Florida, University of West Georgia, Stanford Research Institute International, Medical College of Virginia, and the National Institutes of Health.

DAVID RYBACK, Ph.D. is a consultant and speaker on personal, sports and organizational success working under the banner of EQ Associates International in Atlanta, GA. An active member of the National Speakers Association, his experience encompasses business management and sports consulting, as well as teaching at Emory University's School of Business. His diverse client list includes the National Football League, the U.S. Dept. of Defense, financial institutions, manufacturers—both domestic and international, health care organizations, and national outlets. On a personal note, David runs the 10K Peachtree Road Race every year and holds belts in judo, kenpo karate, and tae-kwon-do. Additional information on his work on emotional intelligence can be found at the EQ Associates website.

WANT TO HEAR MORE ABOUT THE PSYCHOLOGY OF CHAMPIONS?

Dr. Jim Barrell and Dr. David Ryback are consultants and speakers on the topic of the psychology of champions, not only for athletic but for corporate and educational organizations as well. In particular, they can speak on the "how-to" of creating an environment conducive to excellence and success in all realms of competition—athletic, business, or educational.

With a combined experience of teaching at various universities, including the Emory University School of Business and the University of Florida, and consulting with the Orlando Magic, San Francisco 49ers, and San Francisco Giants, both authors train and give keynote presentations on gaining the Focus Edge Success Habit along with emotional intelligence.

To schedule either Jim Barrell or David Ryback for consultation or speaking engagements, please contact David Ryback at 404-377-3588 or David@EQassociates.com for information and availability.